DAYS GOING / DAYS COMING BACK

UNIVERSITY OF UTAH PRESS POETRY SERIES

Other Titles in the Series

Against Paradise
Jonathan Holden
1990

A Day at the Races
Sidney Burris
1989

Snow Water Cove
Jeannine Savard
1988

Headlong
James McKean
1987

Einstein's Brain
Richard Cecil
1986

Early Light
W. S. Di Piero
1985

The Greeting
R. H. W. Dillard
1982

Greenwich Mean Time
Adrien Stoutenburg
1979

An Afternoon of Pocket Billiards
Henry Taylor
1979

The Old One and the Wind
Clarice Short
1973

ELEANOR ROSS TAYLOR

DAYS GOING /
DAYS
COMING
BACK

UNIVERSITY OF UTAH PRESS   SALT LAKE CITY   1991

UNIVERSITY OF UTAH PRESS POETRY SERIES
DAVE SMITH, EDITOR

See Acknowledgments, page 187, for permission statements.

∞ The paper in this book meets the standards for permanence and durability established by the Committee on Production Guidelines for Book Longevity of the Council on Library Resources

LIBRARY OF CONGRESS CATALOGING-IN-PUBLICATION DATA

Taylor, Eleanor Ross, 1920–
    Days going / days coming back and other poems / Eleanor Ross Taylor.
        p.   cm. — (University of Utah Press poetry series)
    ISBN 0-87480-364-0 (alk. paper)
    I. Title. II. Series.
PS3570.A9285D5   1991
811'.54 — dc20   90-48348
                                                                      CIP

CONTENTS

I. Next Year

At the Altar   3

Short Foray   5

In the Echoes, Wintering   7

No Need   8

Harvest, 1925   10

How Morning Comes, Out of Sleep   12

The Greenhouse   13

War Paint and Camouflage   14

Where Somebody Died   18

The Way to Valhalla   19

Mouse   21

A Permanent Dye   22

Maternity Ward   23

Day and Night   24

Vandalized   25

Sleep, after Reading All Evening   26

Lockout Time   28

The Ghost   30

Playing for the Funeral   32

Gainesville, March   34

Rental   35

Dry Nights   37

Haunted   39

Going, Dark   40

Migratory   42

No   44

The Bubble   47

The Sunny Day   48

Enter Daughter   50

Weatherproofing Artemis   51

March 9   52

Roles   53

Waking at Night in a New Apartment   54

Balance Brought Forward   55

On the Writing of Poems   57

Flowers to Your Grave   58

This Year's Drive to Appomattox   60

The Shepherd Strayed   61

Trouble   62

Escaped   63

The Stage Set Painter, 1927   64

The Altar Needlework   67

Breakfast Ascending   69

Hatchways   70

Granddaughter, Christmas   72

The Searchers   73

Boiled Peanuts   74

Pain in the House   75

Grief   76

Dog in *The Quiet Man*   77

One Sort of Heaven   78

Storm   79

Next Year   80

Casting About   82

II. Wilderness of Ladies

The Bine Yadkin Rose   91

Moved   93

Playing   95

Wind   97

Sister   98

Goodbye Family   100

Buck Duke and Mamma   102

Cousin Ida   104

The Chain Gang Guard   107

In the Churchyard   108

Night   109

Woman as Artist   110

Romantic Abstract   112

Out of Habit   114

Song   115

My Grandmother's Virginhood, 1870   116

Motherhood, 1880   117

Family Bible   118

III. Welcome Eumenides

Chapter and Text   125

After Twenty Years   126

The Guard Remembers   128

Welcome Eumenides   129

We Are the Fruit   136

The Skipped Page   137

To a Young Writer   138

The Young Writer's Reply   139

Courtesy Call, 1967   140

Victory   141

Ironweed   144

Sirens   145

One Not Descended   146

Flight   147

Eightieth Birthday   148

Epitaph   149

A Few Days in the South in February   150

IV. In the Bitter Roots

The Painted Bridge   159

The Going Away of Young People   161

Women's Terminal Ward   163

New Dust   164

Rack and Ruin   166

When Robins Return   168

Va. Sun. A.M. Dec. '73   169

Girl in Black-Striped Bathing Suit   170

Limits   171

To Future Eleanors   172

A Little Obituary   174

Over a Stone   175

Love Knows   176

Order and Law   177

New Girls   178

In Case of Danger   179

Rachel Plummer's Dream   181

In the Bitter Roots   184

I

NEXT   YEAR

AT THE ALTAR

That bag you packed me
when you sent me
to the universe —
camp after camp I've opened it
debating whether to unpack —
    Not yet, not yet —
Why did I feel so much in it
was dangerous on the playground,
too good for everyday,
feel those splendid fireworks
hazardous to institutions,
unmannerly to etiquette,
so that, time after time,
I found myself saying
    Not yet?

At each new place I faced it,
it suggested,
Here spread out your things,
put on this coat,
open this bottle —
    No, not yet . . .
sometimes throwing something out,
giving things away,
lightening my load. . . .

The more I pull out,
the more it seems, some days,
is left inside,
the heavier it is.

Sometimes I think this package
is almost a door
the opening of which
careening across heaven
could be fatal.

Some days now I wonder if I'll ever
dare face my given garments —
permanently wrinkled,
surely out of date —
your travel-thought
wasting in its tissue, flesh-corrupt —
till I've absorbed it,
like those stitches that dissolve
in an incision
where something's been removed.

SHORT FORAY

A yellow jacket flew into my taxi
    stopped in traffic near the bank.
It hung between me and the driver,
    feinting indignantly,
    complaining of small headroom
    under the stained blue plush,
    then plunged out to the pickup truck ahead
    and settled on a corner of its bed,
    an amber scab.

My driver never twitched an earring;
    he idled lassitudinously,
    one with the motor; half-dozed,
    seemed not to apprehend
    age and infirmity, imminent bee sting,
    instant allergy and death in twenty minutes.

He was no doubt half-thinking of
    the traffic buzzing both ways,
    the squad car parked beside the bank,
    my tip, his lunch, his weekend —
    sweet circumfluencies.

I had been thinking of
    the present for my granddaughter,
    gift wrapped by an expert, a contrivance
    sure to please a one-year-old,
    the salesman said — while I was hoping
    he didn't see the big spot on my dress
    (discovered on my way over)
    and so withhold the princess wrap
    from a blind old lady and unknowing baby.

Naturally one doesn't remember being one —
     what one liked then, if one knew then —
     not even what one's child liked —
     was she ever one? She likes new knaveries:
     lentil pilaf, home videos.

I didn't say a word about the bee,
     or coffee stain, or what I thought.
When we moved on I lost the yellow jacket,
     lost whether he kept clinging to the truck,
     went to the bank, or soared off over us.
No clue to what he meant, rushing my taxi.
Did he know it was October, bees-up time,
     and take this warm day for a last rich look
     at the boundaries of things, a day of
     stinging a boundary or two if he felt like it,
     playing time bomb?
Did he smell wild asters somewhere in a ditch?
Or did he just ride into town on that pickup
     and mean to go home on it?

IN THE ECHOES, WINTERING

In nice weather we heard them.
They lunched outside,
didn't talk much,
listened to the stereo,
turned it on at least,
to echo off the clapboards.
    We couldn't be sure.
Windows opened. Or doors closed.
The reed fence scrambled in the wind.
    Some days he sounded older.
She never sounded older.
We thought they talked of leaving —
at least one of them —   a droning
as of planes —
or northbound shorebirds —
but that was over
wine in the flush of afternoon,
deep in the bricks the wine
settling vaporish
and if there was
a real bird in the tree,
talk stopped.
    We thought they never knew why.
When they took up again
it was fatigue patched up —
our dissonance,
muffled, but not tuned out,
shivering.

NO NEED

A rain-splashed paper spiked on the gate:
    "No need to finish sweeping the cemetery.
    Mr. Phillips will not be buried here."

A broom lies on the path,
dividing
the swept from the unswept.

Dried sweet-gum balls
that used to swing
when living in the trees —
a knot of wire —   some leaves
charred by disease —
with other oddments
beg pardon, near the broom.

A feeling —
that we can't sweep fast enough.
A feeling that the cortege
passed this way
and Mr. Phillips (unintroduced,
unintroducible) took in
those dried globes,
changed his mind.
Or did a Mrs. Phillips #2?
A feeling
Eunice, Wife of Ralph
possessed the plot?
And the cortege flew on
to some clean sweep.

A feeling
in the paper voice —
How like something else:
No need to stamp the letter;
Mr. Phillips will not call for mail.
An impression —
on the path between
the swept and the unswept:
a pile of brooms,
like swords at a surrender.

HARVEST, 1925

It took two nights to shuck the Hawfields' corn,
    piled, foreskinned, altar high,
        outside the crib.
Lanternlight. Hard trolling motions.
    Dark pent-up communion,
        with supper first, many
women together, in church clothes
    preparing food relentlessly
        as if for some dread rite.
Big Helen Hawfields
    (her long sultry breasts,
        her deep unwilling laugh)
stalked the harvest table,
    lost out the window in
        the high, encroaching winter wind,
the empty calyxes
    of cotton, a spinster's net — (*o*
        do not let the world depart
nor close thine eyes against the night) —
    she filled the lanterns
        trembling, the long wicks heavy
with combustible,
    all the blurred brandy dreams
        in her outskirts
gathered in one drunk longing
    for Tattoo's broad body.
        Below the shuck pile
was a paradise
    lipped by wild plums
        in troubled tangle;

his Maggie found them there,
       stood, hard cheeked, dazed
              at Tattoo's gnashing grin —   back
to the mourners' bench! —
       at Helen's bent-up scuttering,
              weeping, behind the plums,
a lactate field mouse,
       shucks cleaving
              to her teats.

HOW MORNING COMES, OUT OF SLEEP

(It comes) Surprised
on the face of the clock.

    Innocent, night-wise.
    Fisticuffs and running quit,
    changed to repose
    supine on my pillow,
    sleepchatter stilled.

(It comes) Out of dream billow,
whole mansions docked
to my footboards.

    My youth and the dead thereof,
    the farflung thereof,
    distant as jasper shores,
    the smell of a pressed rose.

Griefs lying tranquil,
aches sedated.

    Pale day lighting up,
    a future stated
    in the length
    of an intimate mattress,
    the four walls
    of a room adorned
    with shafts of the world
    projecting through windows.

Singing: *I was born! I was born!*

THE GREENHOUSE

These lofty windows strain the winter light,
    remove its dregs, decant out pain and cold.
Domine refugiam — of the picked survivors,
    though winter's ice and aching are to come,
    for here warmth gathers in a fist,
    the fingers of one family, drawn up
    against destruction, knuckles knelt
    against indomitable season.
Bright in the magic, still, of flowering,
    a small child drops a bead
    on a kneeling-bench; a black veil turns
    with numb, matured, tutorial care.
Under our own glass vaulting
    leaf is still shading leaf,
    limb by deciduous limb.
And he
    who does not share this greenhouse —
    he is with wilder and unluckier things
    gone dormant, flung from the bounded
    centripetal warmth of our sweet, drawn-up ring-around.

WAR PAINT AND CAMOUFLAGE

They always prayed at last.
If not to God, to death.

    The trees are turning again,
    bedding down for winter. . . .
    Our feather bed was getting flat;
    did she find more geese? . . .
    He went round and round on his tether.
    Then the dogs had his bones.

        My children are preparing themselves.
        When I was sick last year.
        In the meantime,
        I ride my stationary bike,
        and stay right here near my doctor.

The chapter began so well.
It was over the hills and far
away, and the stars still out.
Even when, at daybreak,
they appeared on the path,
we were not sure — so unwarlike,
and in their language.

        My contract only stipulated
        there be no transfer,
        and there was none, per se.
        Nobody made a killing. . . .
        Some people are like dogs in money,
        don't know which way to turn,
        guess there's something in it,
        something mysterious, sniffworthy —
        eat some, drink some, bury some.

Five days later it was not
whether there will be any dinner —
the word didn't apply.
We eyed the offal thrown out to the dogs.
We eyed the dogs.
In January the braves couldn't get near game
for the noise of snow-crust breaking;
so it was only some old fox and raccoon bones
boiled till the strings were chewable,
but I did get mine down, and life came back.

    I thought I'd die while she ate that rice pudding;
    there were just four big shrimps in my whole salad.
    But I was down to 125 Wednesday.

— or prayed to death,
i.e., to the old squaw, faced
like the Devil (where had
Squire Knight observed the Devil?) —
who took a board and shovelled
coals onto the Captain's back
after he fell at last
and lay upon his belly.
After he'd gone round and round
on the coals, tethered.
    (If only I had listened to Wawatum!
    Often that winter he had been wakened
    by *the noise of evil birds*.)
Then they scalped him.

    It's the darkness — do you hear it?
    I went and sat out in the yard.
    The moon had great big eyes. It wanted
    to brush against me like a cat.
    Not especially affectionately. . . .
    Pain is what hurts the most. . . .
    Then he stood up again, inside the flames.
    But I think he did not feel pain any more.

Well, the doctor didn't want me to become addicted.
So it was Tantalus all over again, with the Tylenol.
I just went wild around the house at night,
upstairs and downstairs, looking for relief.

Having no shoes against the snow
I stopped and wrapped my feet up in my blanket,
but, growing stiff, and seeing a frozen linnet
under the bushes where I sat, got onto hands and knees,
crawling, I think, several miles, as I thought, east.

During the ice storm
We lost power five whole days.
Soon as they'd fix it, another limb would fall.
People *suffered*.
Nobody keeps a pile of blankets now;
and hundreds of dollars lost in freezer pack,
just when people thought they had something ahead.

They were not strong on landscape,
being captives.
Raising the eyes and looking far
requires a certain off-guard.
Requires if not pleasure in, some
concord with one's status quo.
Mountains were never sublime and
forests did not breathe grandeur;
the rising sun recharged vigilance and the stars
were reproachful for routes lost.

We put these pines in to screen out
their trash cans (of course in summer
air conditioning helps drown out the mowers)
and we bought Tim a telescope he's never used.
Too much city light.
Of course, we love this house.

I keep biting the skin off my lip.
I don't know what I'd be upset about
unless it's that baby yelling Mommee.
You see two people were needed:
somebody to take Dad to the hospital
and somebody to stay with Mom.
That's why it happened —
I couldn't be two people.

Life's no longer simple.
The hunger of the first part
sues the hunger of the second part.

I carry my prayer on a stick:
Over-population is murder.

WHERE SOMEBODY DIED

The self refuses to appear
     in this bare place.
It fears that mute chair
     and the still window.
The sunlight scares it.
There might rise up a sound.
The door doesn't like to move,
     and the crow out there
     hesitates; he knows
     a hole flown into by mistake
     would make a bite of him.
What was sits standstill in the chair,
     hangs, stunned, against the dry-eyed light.
Nobody in sight.
Inanimate things, still lifeless.
This room's so empty
     I doubt I'm standing here;
     there can't be room for me
     and total emptiness.
Only some far-off sounds persist.
The brute truck
     over on the interstate.
The flames in the incinerator
     chewing his old vests.

THE WAY TO VALHALLA

Striding,

the artist on the way to Valhalla
strides,

strides past thin Julie Morisot
and her starved greyhound,
gazing peakedly
as at the camera,
at the omnivorous eye
that looks, devours, snaps shut.

Was there no voice to stay
her mother's
Abraham-uplifted-hand?

To stay vain Serebryakov's
insipid scholar's pen
printing *You can't*
on music in the night,
muting his tender vassals —
striding toward his Valhalla?

No god, clay or pure gold, rejects
fate's singled-out
unblemished man,
tutored in bliss a bit,
climbing up slowly
the teocalli steps,

a ray of sunlight fallen in a pit,

born for the shadows,
for an unmarked grave,
or gnawed bones scattered
on the way to Valhalla.

Odin grant every artist
plaster or sterling
his human sacrifice,
willing, unwilling.

MOUSE

Have pity on this little mouse
    running and hiding,
      the last mouse in the house, and
      slated, she knows, for extinction.
Couldn't she skitter through cupboards
    happy as mouse?
Cat has friends and telephone calls,
    persons to stroke her neck
    and open cans.
Like Puss-In-Boots retired,
    cat catches for diversion.
But — when cat's legally restricted —
    will mouse's hypertension
    really remit?
    and her pathological insomnia?
Who will mouse be?
Cat gives her her identity.
Will mouse prowl by day,
    calling from room to room,
    her walkie-talkie loud on her belt?
Mouse, watch it.
You grow gross claws
    and stalk your neighbors' bassinets.

A PERMANENT DYE

. . . . goats and berries.
  Just when I was thinking of immortality,
      if my daughter had a daughter. . . .

a file of mohair goats
    across a footbridge somewhere,
        and she's begun boiling broomstraw,
plunging fleece in kettles,
    in pots of bark and broomstraw juice,
        the running berries of the ditches,
the bleeding berries of her summers
    spilling their liquid in the stewpot;
        wool and berries,
wool and onionskins,
    the mordant nipping them together,
        a stable color.
She's begun spinning mohair
    clipped from her own flock.
        (Don't worry. It comes back.)

A kid gestates — how many months?
    Lives — how long?
        The running berries of the ditches,
the hurrying weedbloom of her summer,
    moth-mullein and goat's rue,
        moths, fly-by-nights.

(Don't be concerned. The dye is permanent.)
    The newborn scarf falls from the tissue:
        "Like the one, you know, Grandmother had."

MATERNITY WARD

Since the new mother, cross and tired,
    has gone to sleep early,
    he leaves the darkened room,
    and takes the long hall to the nursery,
    past tiny bulbs along the wall
    set just at cut-off distance,
    shadows crocheting them together,
    a milky-blue expanse.

That elevator goes up to the top,
    where people die, he knows,
    where men push muffled mops
    not to wake ears from dying,
    where room lights are turned off,
    maybe forever,
    waiting for the bright blank burst of light
    that comes with death.

Here, in a slumber of creation,
    the pulsing whites reflect all pallors.
Glass panels screen from him
    the soft handfuls of bodies,
    so recently part of another body,
    and still half dormant, on their sterile trays,
    diapered amphibians, panting gently,
    globose.
Vapors and shadows flicker: thin,
    terminal grandfathers vaporizing;
    new nebulae gathering, slowly,
    a maze of motes.
A nurse dreams through her graveyard-shift schedule
    in this time-marriage. Our flesh
    delivers ghosts.

DAY AND NIGHT

It's at daybreak
stars melting fast
I fight
these memories I share with a grave,
memories no one but me
shares with that grave.
Our memories meet,
hers dead and mine alive.
I hold her hand,
                  speak
with my fingers,
still warm, on our memory,
to her fingers pulling,
pulling on their flight
to perfect eclipse,
on me,
almost ready to break
slate-clean with day.

VANDALIZED

Raccoons' dog-smell's still hanging on the air,
    and all my heeled-in cuttings are ripped out.
Here, in the sheltered spot near my bedroom
    (I've killed whole days there with my ear to Brahms,
    whole nights pursuing edelweiss *alpinum*)
    can you believe these tossed-out roots,
    the spit-out styrofoam from potting cups?
They've dunked their garbage in my fountain,
    where Cherub's poised on classic toe
    as if to pour into the larvaed shell,
    and used my mulch for litterbox;
    scratched jeers across the tags —
    "Road Narrows"? "Blasting Zone"? —

       Cuttings I ordered weeks ago,
to sheets of Brahms,
before I made my mind up to leave here,
gave up new planting, lost interest in
white, noble, mountainous,
took steady work, slept well
and never dreamed I was raccoons.

SLEEP, AFTER READING ALL EVENING

This house was built by Trollope.
You feel at home.
You know the footman,
    a relative of Mini-Maid and Domino's.
Become a gentleman,
    you set your man's hat on the floor,
    as earmark of the drop-in call.
At the dance, you know them all —
    who's waltzing blindly
    with Burgo, her girl's embedded dream?
(The young Duke's wife, the carriage gone already
    to fetch her lord: *But I do love you, Cora.*)
As if his love could ever be enough.
And lofty Nidderdale is being kind —
    his nature —
    to lost Marie, off to the Melting Pot.
As if kindness could be enough.

One French door's open on
    the Pemberley Prospect,
    Jane's wily walks.
One shower's over. Lucky —
    you've lost your raincoat.
Here, moving toward you inescapably,
    libido in the flesh —
    Darcy, the longed-for body,
    in morning clothes.
Will he speak?

You find yourself
    back in her robber glen, her keep.
Years have gone; she has forgotten me, and
    I have half forgotten, yet at this hour
    I feel that I am face to face with fate —

that deeper-than-life urge,
programmed within, looms
from its depths.

But the wind's up on the moor,
and in the windows at the Grange,
sudden extinction; enlightenment blows out,
our pages turning by fits
quickly in a loosening gust.

As if paper could ever be enough;
Barabbas walking free;
our master waked in chains.

LOCKOUT TIME

Around us are the young,
    carousing from their dormitories.
But we are off to Florida,
    packing the house, slow motion,
    shuffling forgotten things —
    things stolen from us long ago,
    loved, unneeded things —
    wood carvings of triceratops,
    Christmas tree swans,
    bright and sibylline.
I want to take this book of tapestries.
I might make one.

A bearded, fat buffoon delays us,
    singing and scratching himself.
I snap at him, and everybody smiles.
I'm 70, I plead.
I have to get off early.
We all rise.

Out, down the halls, toward bed.
Out, between buildings and up steps —
    stone steps, a hard flight.
Moving with the students,
    young, exhilarated, late at night.
3 A.M. I, faint, hungry for my pillow.

But I don't have my Florida house key.
As luck would have it.
I turn back, toiling.
Down the stairway,
    the whole flight empty now.

I see the proctor at the bottom.
She's locking up.

May I go get my key? I call.
But the door's been locked.
She smiles and shakes her head. No.
As if it doesn't matter. No.
And there're the stairs to climb,
    there's pitiless hospital gloom.

THE GHOST

Our paterfamilias
was an elusive guy.
   (Maybe he didn't like children?)

Don't think
I ever heard him say
ten words together
though we were together
in the world ten years.
He was always
behind his mustache   or
in the other room   or
sitting in the front yard
tolerating his sons-in-law   or
gone to town.

(The money gone
with Uncle Joe to Mississippi,
the land gone with
the gobbling rains, the gobbling cotton.)

   But now sometimes
   I sit death-still
   (resurged small
   in a braked rocking-chair)
   remember hard,
and he comes forth on his back porch,
a stocky, pulpy man with tattered eyes,

picks up his loose black hat
parked on the bucket shelf,
takes down his rubbed shotgun,
and ramrod straight descends the wavy steps,
pausing to pick a feather off his sleeve
and flick it far.

He moves on past the barn, the exiled sycamore,
and towards the running river.

A hound ears-up and
passions after.

They disappear.

PLAYING FOR THE FUNERAL

Humoring slight voices pianissimo,
    she's accompanied four preachers' wives
who featured themselves solo.

This apse that even with no coffin misgives
    the heart, lures her two days a week
to practice its one bright positive.

Children, fleshed to their mothers' hands, go peek
    into the faceshells of the wife and child
laid in one casket, in the one sunstreak,

this one-of-three daylights of the child.
    As Kate strict-times the ill-timed "Shadows Flee,"
beyond the ruffled gladiola piles

a harrowing noise, a goon hilarity,
    comes from the family huddled at the front;
their shudders might be comedy.

Before it's over, one will, likely, faint.
    (When Brad died — thirty-five! young Brad's age now —
she left the boys at home — her errant

style. His mother too she spared somehow. . . .
    Life's full . . . her pupils . . . Mother's care. . . .)
The choir, tear-blinded, Kleenex-gagged, breaks down.

Only the pianist perseveres.
    Tactfully covering sobs, she
keeps the place, humming to her own ear,

her metronome: *Hail, Death! and Open, Gates!*
    till dead and live are finally dismissed.

She shelves the requiem and abdicates;
    Honda fullspeed home, spots eighty-year-old Bess
sweeping her porch. Glancing idly hearse-wise,
                    slows down,

toots, *Hi there! Hi there! Me, too, Miss Bess!*

GAINESVILLE, MARCH

A rain of robins.
Sheets.
Nobody was expecting them —
    not I, limboed in 85 degrees.
Not cat, washing stand-by feet
    in idle ablution; no one told her
    to clean between her claws today
    for spring.
She strains to track, above her,
    beeping wings, wings beeping crazily
    a Virginia backyard, beeping imperatively
    trees, slothfully ungreen, up the coast.
She sighs, leaps to her windowsill,
    locks up her eyelids to this foreign sun;
    sees, still, birds dipping, falling,
    filling yards, birds leafing out
    on fronds and fence,
    spring-wound, with time's-up wings.
Somewhere March sun's an iced, coronaed daffodil. . . .
She's in her carrier, trekking I-95. . . .
Panting a little, eyes shut,
    we *Exit North*.
Our homesick claws dream-drive.

RENTAL

When she wrote the check
        she accepted exorbitance.
That address came high —
        though small, right on the water,
        its own landing, three bedrooms,
        walled garden, CAC.
In this heaven there'd be everything:
        fish untold in the inlet,
        cocaine smugglers,
        strange birds, mysterious calls,
        high carat sunlight beamed
        straight up the stairs —
        everything, everything.

She made herself privy
        to their photo album:
        the yellowed Just Marrieds,
        and the ancients newly photographed;
        privy to their king-sized mattress
        wed to scant queen blanket.
Why were his books
        beside the guest-room bed?
The perfect sheets,
        remarkably, had her own initials,
        just scrambled.
                All hers. Her AliBabaiad.

She waked — to a motor's scream? —
        in the stiff monograms
        unreadable by midnight,
        waked still in dream,
        clinging to her cuddled berth,
        yearning, petted, dream-enchanted
        in the soothing inexorable, exotic
        arms of that phantasmal landlord,

his pallid, paid-up eyes on her
hypnotic,
his walker within reach,
his gray mouth to her ear:
    my love my love —

The blood-sucking
    sharks, oh the vipers.

DRY NIGHTS

In the dry dusk,
safe, soundless lightning,
their hope of rain,
flashed in the west,
flicked at the August porch,
and then receded
writing silently,
a snaking pencil
on clouds miles away.

Schoolgirls, we
detached us from them, we
charged insistently
from lamps and porch,
charged blackness,
ordered a terra nova
through the unmapped clouds,

while they
sat in the young dark,
one in the swing,
one back to column,
disclosing twosome what they'd thought,
all day, one in the house,
one far afield:
some unearthed atom of their childhoods,
some brooded yield,
some duet silence,
casting, now and then
into the dark:
    Don't go too far.
    Don't stumble on a snake.

Rain never came, as I remember —
never comes,
and we, most lost,
are compassed looking back
at those two sitting there
half darkness and half lightning
in our night.

HAUNTED

Can I decide between apple and oak,
plotting a future of shadow and shade?
    My mother sits rocking rocking rocking
    singing *Faith is the victory*

(Don't do that) I whisper. She doesn't hear,
    even with her multiple rocking ears.
    I rattle my spade.

I read about oaks. Holm, chestnut, hybrid.
Some achieve eighty feet with equal spread.
    She sits rocking, *Faith is the victory*

I leave my books and spade.
News, then? Chopin? The skull
constantly gapes ahead. Except hers, dead.
    Faith faith is the victory

I walk outside. . . . Horse-apple? Pippin?
the birds are clacking, upset:
the feeder empty!
something stalking! cat!

I sprawl in the sun,
the shutter of my lids,
the shutter of my skull,
drawn.
Through pulsing jalousies
sun's ultra hum:
    O
    glorious victory
    of faith
        of faith
    that overcomes

GOING, DARK

He

She sees that he comes and goes.
He leaves the room,
steps back again.
But he is still Guard.
He is preparing to go. Bored
with the doors of this ward,
living only, now,
his own death row,
he hardly watches her.
He's packed,
pared to essentials,
his heartpulse faint,
his protoplasm slack,
his charge tripping to bolt.
   Come dark, he'll go.

She

She's been a long time packed,
old lashed-up vistas
stealthily unchained;
her heartpulse, too,
caught in his haste,
half gone.
       She shakes out
a green extrinsic flag to dry,
plays drowsing on her cot.
Come dark, I'll fly.
Her nails bite at her voltaged flesh:
   I'm not through with it yet. . . .

It

Dark
in its cell of stars
wheels,
a falling of blocks:
dulls of negligence,
dooms of release,
dooms of pardon,
tombs of indifference.

MIGRATORY

Last year I hesitated
    even to acknowledge it. My old roommate,
    and it was meant to be a fun visit.
But the tuft of feathers
    was still clinging to the window
    there where guests always sit.

In the days before she came
    there had been three —
    a jay, a catbird, and a young phoebe.
I thought it was the leaves going,
    letting more light down on the panes.
That, and the time of year, the urge for fugue
    that even in winter residents
    sometimes sends them hellbent
    into blind depth and distance.

"Just throw a cup of water on them.
    They come right to. I do it all the time.
    They just fly off."
Glad, as always, to pass on a tip.
We knew, then, her prognosis,
    but she felt okay between treatments,
    could say, "I've got to call Clarice —
    she'll think I'm gone!"
She said again, "Just try it."

    But I can't bring myself to.
    I've heard the thud; looked at the soft lump,
        wings-down on the steps outside,
        eyes shuttered, body heaving.
    But — douse a thing half dead?
    If it died before my eyes?

She planned the simplest service,
    and went down by herself to pick the coffin
    (they sent a man out for her) —
    surprisingly, one soft blue, robin's egg —
    like something she'd picked out to wear,
    not to be caught, like me,
    without a decent garment to put on.

NO

Who will meet her?
    sitting ahead of me,
    her face a crushed girlskin,
    her head rotating
    almost acceptably, as if she were
    just looking out west windows of the bus,
    then out east ones and back,
    a run of negatives — ?
Has her world changed out-and-out?
Or has she lived bound to some weird set-up —
    the mule that's dragged the wheel
    till it can only circumscribe,
    and at a straight path must be led?

What doctor sanctioned this furlough?
Can she be circling alone?

Her hair, an edgeless haze.
Under the cotton shell, a stance
    wandlike, almost airborne.
She rises now and then compelled
    to seem to look out windows,
    her face unseeing; frets with
    her large dark purse and, at her feet,
    black plastic trash bag with twist tie.

Within her trance she's spotted
    free seats across from me;
    deserts a sleeping Mexican,
    taking her plastic bag,
    to sit alone.

Her garment's flowered; her soles
    inside flat sandals, old rubber
    weathered to chapped rose.
She takes off twist-it, rapt;
    opens the bag, peers in,
    cautiously shifting things, removing nothing,
    arm elbow deep, like one engaged in calving;
    takes out — can it be, more folded plastic bags
    blistered with use? . . . *Not those.*
And something coarse and white — dish towels?
Change of underwear? *Not that.*
She is alone, absorbed
    she's in some way-off house,
    a mansion long devoid of lords;
    or a big empty room
    with towering windows —
    even a small empty room —
    alone, so alone one wonders
    where she is going TO, who
    has room enough for that loneliness, that quiet.
Yet —   not where she is going,
    but where she came from —

Now she slides out a worn,
    staghandled paring knife.
The thin blade's longish.
She drifts it out and puts it by,
    restores the bags and piece of cloth,
    fastens the twist-it patiently,
    then moves back to the Mexican.
By now he's taken over her seat, too.
She almost sits on him.
He jumps awake, his look a reprimand.

Remotely. . . . 'cuse. . . . Then
    her being seems to vanish.
Her head repeats its back-and-forth.
The knife rides in the seat across from me
    in independent menace.

I check the other passengers,
    the ones who turn and eye her anxiously,
    for one in charge of her.
Perhaps the Mexican's her keeper.
He seems to feel no threat.
Abruptly she investigates her skirt,
    looks quickly backward to the seat she left,
    not rising, reaches back,
    arm stretching crazily
    till like a magnet it's pulled in the knife.
She draws it to her lap, sits straight (*that's done*)
    becomes again the metronome
    that drums no tune —
    no
    no
    no

THE BUBBLE

Bubbles powder the steps.
Back steps project into abyss,
    out into nothingness,
    down to a panful of infinity's gray tears,
    a round gray probe of soapy water.
On the top step, tears of nothingness —
    that wept themselves dry
    in a bleak canyon of dry wrinkles,
    of liver spots, of melanoma
    benign, not even lethal —
    sit, played out.
On the bottom step, the toddler, bare feet
    on the grass.
Her toes, not meaning to,
    press down time's button,
    the one that restarts nothingness,
    the one that reruns gray infinity.
Her round heels hold their breath,
    winnowing bubbles,
    these shells of water momentary,
    guile of colored light,
    gray moonstone tears
    of loss and irrecovery.
One human-fist-sized bubble,
    a little more significant,
    hangs back, hangs near them,
    bragging existence,
    gathers its colors to itself, then
    rises, perfectly, up in the trees,
    over the roof.
But where it went,
    and whether it found the nature of its existence,
    neither of them pursues.

THE SUNNY DAY

Suddenly, it's dark. Since noon
    from my desk I've watched
    two boys play at rescuing
    a gosling gone over the pond dam
    into my creek, detached
    from his goose tribe
    by street and culvert.

I heard his startled cheep
    eluding them time after time;
    their childish disappointed cries.
I almost called to them:
    The alligator sleeps there.
But the sun was saying otherwise.
And, of course, they knew.

Resting from the typewriter,
    I watched, across the street,
    young couples walk babies
    and adopted dogs around the pond,
    puppies twinkling on a leash
    in the new sun.

A paper picnic in a pickup
    tossed scraps out to the long-necked geese
    sailing the pond starchily,
    examples of and to
    non-accident-prone issue.
I worked on, withdrawn
    in my inside reflections.

Suddenly, it's quiet.
Dogs and babies gone, picnickers gone.
Dark. I turn my light on
and get up to close the door and
    pull the drapes, being alone in the house.

Up from the creek's curbstones
    in the inching dark
    the gosling's crying,
    loud and articulate,
    to vanished pond,
    to pond's reflections of the sky,
    to sun, to the thermometer —
    articulate and loud —
    it strikes me,
    peculiarly a grown goose cry.

ENTER DAUGHTER

Plumped with 10 P.M. feeding
    she's poked in by her
        mother-in-sweater-and-Keds.
He's at his reading,
    his desk the one ember
        left burning in hid domestic shade.
On the closet door one
    vestigial hardrock poster
        vibrates still;
his cigarette smokes on;
    his drink waits
        on its makeshift coaster.
He sets her on his palm.
    She fills the adroit dish
        woven of stabled muscles.
(Was it for this he strangled hobo wishes?)
    He supports the rotating neck
        and graceless diaper;
eyes the mysterious bluff
    of her pristine stare,
        tickles, cooly, the shapeless cheek,
the gaping lip, and bare feet
    (angled red nymphal imperatives).
        Her milky eyes narrow with mirth.
A miniature laugh
    springs from the original book of laughs;
        she shakes; her eyes water;
red digits rise and fall with laughter;
    then, stiffening her pink girth,
        she gives him a straight look.

WEATHERPROOFING ARTEMIS

It may be it's too late.
Who would have thought
    two weeks of terrace life
    would age her in this way,
    her chalk head finely riddled,
    cheeks eaten by birdlime?
It may be her soft plaster
    will still collapse
    in some downpour.

My brush torments
    the knifedrawn curls
    skeined up for bygone sprints.
Here's where my catbird at her ear,
    the raccoon dabbler in my birdbath
    picked at the bound-up hair,
    the shoulder pin,
    the arteries in the neck.

My brush offends the blind eyes,
    afeeling mouth, and knuckled chin,
    and struck by twilight
    I reel back from
    the sticky cunning head
    staring behind me,
    unloose her to the night.

From indoors I can just make out
    my offering, primed for new life,
    set on the black-shawled garden's doorstep.
She hovers evanescent
    under the Bradford pear,
    my city tree,
    damning my planting
    gauged for high tech care,
    then lifts a vaporous sandaled heel:
    Flight now departing.
    Weather fair.

MARCH 9

Such days as this it rains in Norwood.
March. The wind whistles under its breath
as that woman did, sewing. Afraid of — ?
    Yes, it's surely raining in Norwood cemetery.
But here, in the dry shrubbery, bloom's opiate,
the Key West marl rejects the dead,
breezes erase, erase, and the slate's clean.

    — No. It reads March 9, 1910.

    The buggy bumps smartly
    along the polished clay.
    Under the laprobe hands fuse.

    They lie together.
    No water floats them out,
    the walls a hardened cavity.

       A little wet snow fell this day.

    The same starved hyacinths
    rise up among the weeds.
    Some backwoods hand will pillage.
    Breath her-age-then will gulp the still rich smell.
    The wine seeps on from bulb to bulb.
       Her fluid hand enhanced.
       Her radiance broke up dormancy.

All dead hands are the same age: dead.
I note my own.
Last year, trembling,
they harvested hyacinths
for the graves' navels.
Has no one cleared away
that dessication at the stones?

Another dessication comes.

It rains. The rain is young.

ROLES

Woman-like (I was told)
    ignoring snow shovels,
I took one from the hearth
    to spoon a path shoe-wide
    out to the gate.
I resented the whole thing —
    snow, and the temperature, and
    the wind picking at my hat,
    and the weight — the dead-weight enormity
    of the flashy, fiendish stuff;
    above all, the cardinal in the hemlock
    complaining like a baby,
    instead of one of nature's wildlings,
    about water frozen
    and worms below the ground below the snow,
    and bugs burrowing deeper under the bark —
Hard work, hard work, he fussed,
    eyeing me as if he had the shovel, and
    I was a peck of snow.

WAKING AT NIGHT IN A NEW APARTMENT

Whether I care to live,
on another planet?

Whether the same laws hold?
Of gravity.

What will tie me,
home-gone,
to anything pretold?

Are books books, floors floors?
Are there still ends to roads?
How can I gravitate
from this cold height,
straggling across the sky,
trudging over trees,
climbing down sending-towers,
not a parachute in sight?

Even my caul would be welcome.
Especially my mother's house.

I bed in this black hour,
a comma in a jar of ink,
pending.

A 16-wheeler wallops by,
drubbing the walls.
(Without pictures, walls
run to their own length.)
A crazy out there in the alley bawls —
he's asking me —
Why'd my bitch die?
R-r-r! Why'd she die?

BALANCE BROUGHT FORWARD

She left, just plain out left,
and left him
that freight of money —
not tons,
but much from her.
Astonishing, she was money.
Sitting by her cot he'd never thought
she was money,
she was real estate,
she was clocks and cows
and barns and policies.
But here it was,
piled up around him,
crept into his pockets,
burdening the mail.
In college,
getting the chipped-edged dollar bills
in "linen" envelopes,
remembering the henhouse,
the cream mill's loaves-and-little-fishes bones
sunning on the back porch bench
under the hanging galvanized milk pails,
considering, over *Elements of Business*,
her minus pocketbook, her silence,
he hadn't calculated this.
He never caught on to
that deal she made:
I'll give, you take.
Sitting beside her
in Room 20B —
her skimpy covers,
blotted gown,
odor of cheap beef on her plate,
her steady non-binding gaze
never prepared him.

She must have sweated some,
figuring, re-filling his sock,
before her getaway.
He ran a red light,
speeding after,
adding it up, outdone —
No! Wait! You shorted me!

ON THE WRITING OF POEMS

I want my bed

where the seeds of day
sprout, leaf out,
bloom in a black prolixity
all night.

I want my sleeping pill.
I want the ladders and
the fans of wings
or of photos.

I want that shutterflux
that in the morning is
the light tax
that's it's own scrip:
that pays me for the smell
of bacon in the frying pan,
defrays all day
a dying capital.

I think of staying
in this bed from now on,
redeeming venal daylight,
till my last day comes down
over my smoking rinds,
a splendid, domed,
reflecting, skillet lid.

FLOWERS TO YOUR GRAVE

The jasmines by the steps,
    that daughters on the front porch,
    diligently idle,
    their poems on the swing's arms,
    swung to the sweet of,
    while you ironed on the dining table,
    or pedalled stitches in the hall —

those jasmines have been moved
to the old shrub row,
with trunks unpruned.
    Passing them, you'd recognize
    their birth defects —
    knobbed stems, uneven angles.

    And the peony's the same blood-hoard,
    tight-fisted, not to waste
    its poor dirt budget.
    Its one excess, that red.

    When you came, a bride —
    only moss-splotched oaks
    wedged in bedrock.

Today, as you don't come
to your wild made-up park,
I take it,
    in a jar that's held
    kraut or sweet pickles.
    I take descendants of your jasmines
    and your Jacob's ladder —
    a flimsy flight,
    its throated purple steps
    dying, downstairs up,
    into a frontier heaven.

We leave the driveway.
　　Here your sphere ended;
　　your eyes lit secretly
　　at this abroad,
　　home shackles sprung:
　　President Hoover, Bishop Marr,
　　running water and electric lights,
　　out here somewhere.

Today the gates are open
for some reason. The usual reason.
There is just enough passing
to keep these lanes lanes,
enough to keep the world
pruned to life-size.

I set my offering down:
　　Take yours,
　　of you.
　　This I picked for you.
　　Take and remember.
　　Eat of them
　　in that after-garden.

Through the clay
a blue ruelle's pushed up;
a drop of water's wobbling in its cup.
I blink.
Dust blows, across the foretold grass.
A birth of ruelles runs out
from your grave,
a string of blue firecrackers
popping over every mound to
edge and end of this dead-ground,
fiesta-firing.

THIS YEAR'S DRIVE TO APPOMATTOX

March comes,
and Eastern bluebird shows himself,
a long-awaited call, on the telephone wire,
    Confederate blue and old blood.

Make a fist. Okay Hold up your arm
like that a minute or two.
You'll have the lab report next week.
    If you still like mortality.

We go past church and stones, genesis, exodus.
That house played house to many bones;
these fields, to hoof and brogan,
    that hilltop woods to wind.

Wind whips her dress against her legs,
under the clothesline, taking down the ghosts.
It's cold. They aren't whipped out by wind,
    our ghosts — they drive the wind.

A future's hatching out of firmament,
an Oberland, and 1865 is drying mist —
        and last year,
what recollection has last year —
    two, not one, here?

THE SHEPHERD STRAYED

(The Rev. Lewis Lunsford, 1753–1793,
   Morattico Church, Va.)

Your double-bed-sized slab
flat on the grass
lines out your facts
and then fades off
soliloquizes,
choked with fungi:
    he died away from home
    at the house of
    mr. gregory of exeter

Since 1793 these useless
everlasting bones
have taken you nowhere.
These bones without you,
these bones without
the willing muscle
your will ruled
in fleshly, sacerdotal you
traveling earthly rounds,
that knelt and knelt,
and,
wandered from the fold,
did perhaps over-dine
at Mr. Gregory's in Exeter —
did perhaps overtax
the holy flesh
that guarded bones,
did perhaps overfire
the you,
the flesh that is not here,
but lives, a nimbus,
ingloriously away from home.

TROUBLE

I still love my garden
  but some fiend's let a viper loose in it.
I keep on working there, of course.
It must be weeded, just for auld lang syne,
  and if not clipped the vines get out of hand.
I work as if I'm hobbled, eyes on the steppingstones.
Some days I do cut phlox,
  nudging with my hoe, pulling back the leaves,
  looking down narrowly
  before I snip.
I find my heart pounding.
I don't spend much time looking at effects —
  too busy watching.
I even lay out heathen tidbits —
  limp pilose life I hate to touch —
  dropped inconspicuously,
  like slow-answered words,
  available, yet out of sight.
Of course I know it's there.
Even after it's eaten there's a stench
  and stain under the fragrant phlox
  of one of those grim blights
  that block new growth, and sicken stems,
  and out-live host.

ESCAPED

Our neighbors' three-legged brindled cat is gone.
They rescued her, a kitten, in a pink shoebox.
She loved cashews, they said.
And newt and frog, I thought —
    we live in mouseless houses on this street.

I used, back late from some tame party in my neighborhood,
    to catch her in the headlights, midstreet,
    three feet ready set, eyes lawless.
And, picking up the paper, mornings now and then,
    my Oomphies planted on the aged-brick walk,
    I'd jump her like a rabbit, in the ivy —
    in sight of home, but chewing feral night.
Yet home was always where she raced, no time-of-day for me,
    as I made for my kitchen and imperative caffeine.

I saw her treed once by a passing tom:
    a Grendel's Mother with some naive rake —
    she wasn't just your sweetheart cat;
    no pairing her with odd-man dinner mates.
Yet now the troubled notice in my door: CAT MISSING,
    its desperate letters dodging in my bills and catalogs:
    CAT MISSING — HAS THREE LEGS.

THE STAGE SET PAINTER, 1927

The school-truck fetched them in
 from foolish outposts on cowpaths
  through red dust and red mud for
   books, eight months per capita.

Two Baby Rays barged in
 the auditorium doors:
  a strange performance
   pulled them to the stage.
Its set-up scenery was half
 white canvas, half bright woods —
  a woods that might be spring or fall,
   with seasons' entry-exit yellows,
a touch of red that might be maple keys,
 and some trees bare — already shed?
  or not yet leafed?

A foreigner, some
 unknown sort of being
  beginning to turn gray
   and thicken at the waist —
was lost in it.
 He started, glowered out
  front-row.
   "Get out. No kids in here."

But out, they cracked the door again,
 eyes rapt till Lonzo rang the bell,
  and next day crept in at recess
   and edged back up the dreary aisle.

Green and yellow, green and yellow.
    The twisted strokes
            brought forth — they made a tree,
                made woods, as if the sun
were shining — made sun —
    as if the wind blew —
            the dabs tricked out the wind —
                wind pulled out from a tray.

"I told you kids, get out."
    "We want to watch an Artist."
            He swore, as if they jeered him,
                at the canvas hatefully;
stabbed on some red and purple,
    more green, more green,
            a Van Gogh tantrum. (Little they knew!)
                They held their breath.

But when he did the room flats,
    a blue just deeper than Wedgwood
        (Little they knew.)
            with parchment mantel and door frames,
                they drifted off. It was too like
                    Tom Dodd, the town housepainter.

"I'm paid no princely wage!"
    he bawled out once. (Little they knew!)
            He slapped it on, to knock off
                the trite drop curtain
(boxes miming Main Street's stores)
    itched to spell in the credits, say
            his Southern come-down done.

"Your materials, now
　　your lumber and your paint —
　　　　That's where's your investment,"
　　　　　the principal explained
　　　　　　　to clerks and merchants.

In the first operetta
　　there were dancing magpies.
　　　　And still, when Baby Rays
　　　　　were almost Hero-sized,
the cowpath fathers
　　clapped up the village curtain,
　　　　still waited raptly the bright kiss
　　　　　of all blown sun, illusive fields,
all language unlike speech:
　　Act II. Scene I. A Wood Near Athens.

THE ALTAR NEEDLEWORK

She who created
    sits, she mollusks somewhere,
sits in a family room
    on Herring Creek,
in front of Nature or
    Your Wild America, sits
postparturient from these her creatures;
    but she's abstracted here,
by no means here,
    not in this empty one-room church
all whirling arches; altar replenished
    with thick wool palette-stitches;
her fat wool stitches crosses,
    double crossed.

In the image of her Creek
    she fashioned them:
beatified blotched frog,
    the feathered Red, the paper yellow wings.
Inviting knees: fall on
    the Herring pine-skeins
fine as shad bones;
    fall on the bristly pink
azalea's microsporophyll:
    bury your knees in pardon,
adoration,
    mute hosanna.
Just missing is the quail's
    voice and the chirp of creek;
but they're not far; half in the air,
    my snail's horns listening
here in this church inherited.
    The pattee cross
aloft hangs,
    ethered up.
The passion flower
    irrays out its nails.

She used her eyes up,
    these envisaging:
the pepper on the robin's chin,
    the minnow's slippy scales,
egg pollen on the bee's foot. She
    callused needled fingers
making, making.
              He
snipped her off
    and cut her out
and wove her thus
    a small and female thing
blue eyed, fine-fingered. . . .
          Him they call Father:
I taken my blue eyes from him,
    my making hands, no doubt.

BREAKFAST ASCENDING

Sleepless,
    lean on your windowsill,
down to blacked-out grass,
    out to moping trees.
The moon's making no noise;
    it's thrown hush-sheets over the street,
over the sung-out birds,
    over the chastened blues, reds, blues,
over your fasting hopes.

But something wideawake evolves
    affectionately on the air:
the smell of bacon.
    Bacon, cooked at all hours.
Hours in your past —
    somebody calling a taxi,
flying to San Francisco;
    a doctor back from late call;
a small boy drowsing to his paper route.

And hours in your future —
    somebody starting on a fishing trip,
somebody waking to a birthday,
    somebody too happy to sleep —
        coming to see you.

HATCHWAYS

Sleeping rapidly
      I climb desperately
      a hatchway mercilessly
      narrow-channeled. . . .
      or else a slimy chimneypot
      my toehold crumbling
      as I twist up

      that offers,
      (if I get through)
               a fatal ledge
      hung over deluged plains,
      no roads there, sea snapping —

Where did this terror come from?
this twitching like despair?
I whose birth was
"the easiest one"
who came fast and simply — I
have no need for such nightmares.

Did some drowned sailor
drifting in race memory, on
some not-as-yet-known electrothought,
chance up in me,
rebuking his hard fate?

Or some wretch in my family past,
too far back for my tale-tellers
to reach back to, come navigate
my sleep,
and wring his trauma out?
rise jinni in my blood?
say that he's me?

Or is that
soon-to-be-born
blood of my blood,
two hundred miles away,
gathering his-or-her strength
(mixed with mine)
on the private, drowsy
sea of amnion,
something like thought
disturbing its red cobweb:
    No choice now.
    Only the job that all flesh must —
he-or-she summoning
our strength for being hurled
through the dread channel to
the raw bite of the world?

Or a black foreshadow
of my shade,
me waking blind
inside strange blood
next century,
mute,
laboring to get the ear
of some deaf, stubborn,
all-enclosing metamorph:
I'm here, here ?

GRANDDAUGHTER, CHRISTMAS

You dolls, bears, big stuffed cats,
stand back, stand clear
of her pink skittering bassinet.
Don't lure her with enamel,
with your inhuman cheer,
your glittering, depthless,
unperceptive eyes.
She sees through your stare.

Wreaths, sheathe in
your wild green spines,
or make sure they're too dull
to draw one drop of blood
from the little cupful
that ventures womanhood.

Gruff drums, call up
your GI Joes.
Discharge the lot
for her lifetime —
pensions for good behavior,
pay doubled for bad shots.

Big candy canes,
hint no infirmity;
twirl, twirling on
into infinity — O
top-hat-dancing
blazon
our small reverberation.

THE SEARCHERS

We loved-and-promised-others.
It was not enough.

Pressed against the deck rail
we broke all promises — if hearts, too bad.
Yet it was not enough.

Kiplinged past Chinese bandits,
smuggling a bonsai trunk,
dissecting the Oriental body —
was not enough.

We came home,
threw out everything
but children's books
and a serving girl with braids;
built our cottage in old apple trees,
dressed formally,
drank with the wittiest,
fought power. Asked afterwards,
in the dark, Is it enough?

An evening bulleting with rain —
carlights
crashed in my lap —

a slick red steering wheel —
you driven through the film
that always hung
between us and enough —
enough.

BOILED PEANUTS

A stretch of country woods,
disfeatured by a roadstand
seething smoke.
Black dress and flying hair
hint, *not farm folk*.
She wipes her hands
as if she dealt in blood.

No telling what goes in this pot
besides peanuts. The water's black —
or is that just the pot? —
looks thick, looks hot —
just hot enough to grow ptomaine?
Or do I smell Clorox?
No telling what.

No telling what goes underneath this pot.
Behind the stand's a furtive heap —
scrap wood, gray nubs of hulls, and pants —
things brought by rain, despair, and rot
to just the topsy-turvy
for rats' sleep.

      "Run out of sacks!"
She takes a dipper
off a monstrous hook,
tips my dank treat
into an old bread bag
and wrings it shut, then
throws my filthy bill a queasy look.

PAIN IN THE HOUSE

Feeling her head pick up her body,
    question mark,
    blurred misstamped question mark
    snakes out of bed,
    trying to jiggle unhappiness
    as little as possible,
    not to wake pain,
    not to raise a shade,
    if raising a shade in the dark wakes pain.
Under the shade the stars are awake, smiling —
    ready to frown on unhappiness.
And the happiness of the unconscious
    is scurrying already
    from the knife-edge of light,
    pain's night-light,
    waiting under the door across the hall.
Dread's square hair stiffens,
    her feet have corners,
    trying to trick the stairs out of their creaking,
    and the house out of groaning before coffee,
    before resurrection.
Death before resurrection is hard;
    breakfast and the stars belong first;
    plenty of time to die all day
    when everything does groan, and unhappiness
    shakes itself out like a musty old mare
    all over the house.
Dread says to herself: Serves me right
    for leaving home, for learning to read;
    serves me right for children and menopause
    and cosmetic surgery, and elation in gin.
          I must travel back
    through the shade and the black holes and the frowns,
    through drink and tampon and alphabet
    to the kitchen and mother and dad and
    the morning of the resurrection was the first day.

GRIEF

    Take my love to heaven
    A waste of love
    spilt   poured out and gone

I hook cups on the shelf.
They could be stacked conveniently,
asleep in one another, not alone.

The books touch and support.
The light shifts for itself,
drains to the heap of personal effects
left to the floor;
the vacant travelling bags,
turned to a fleet
of hearses headed for the attic.

I take a bed sheet,
tear it up for rags,
one, two, three, four!
And each rag is that grief,
drenched with bad fortune.

    Take my love to heaven
    A waste of love
    spilt   poured out and gone

DOG IN *THE QUIET MAN*

Still from the negative
you positively live;
you wag your vulgar tail,
kick at a flea,
intently snuff that other dog.
John Wayne's dead, his stiff leg gone,
McLaglen and Maureen.
Did you give up the ghost,
stretched by some road,
coiled under some scuffed bed? —
you, still a second in
time-margin where life ticks,
and false mortality
reels up an Irish dog
at no time at a loss
at how to spend an hour? —
will meet a train,
go with a crowd,
sit by a chair.
The old flick flicks.
I watch for you.
Here comes the train:
a minute's innocence;
a corner of a frame;
missed by a whisker.
The story never was about you, mutt.

ONE SORT OF HEAVEN

For a while I'll live on
    in the heads of those who lived with me,
For a while I'll come back
    in the dreams of farflung people
    who don't above all want to see me
    ever again
    or think of me,
    my failings,
    or make me live and move
    and look at them,

    as Miss Magnhilde Anders
    moved and looked at me directly
    in my dream —
    sitting in her office
    at the Woman's College,
    desk glassy as the table
    her advisees were asked to,
    once a year, lump sum, to dinner —
    huge Miss Anders rubbing her red wig
    over her clammy forehead,
    her glasses crustacean sockets,

    as she slashed-in
    my hours on a chart,
    directing me, her green advisee:
    study
    three hours of Gibbon in the afternoon,
    three hours of Latin in the evening,
    three hours of Shakespeare Sat. A.M.
    (week-ends not working in the dining hall)
    and make Phi Beta Kappa —
    dreams come to nothing,
    though I admired her pin,
    and her doubtful eyes,
    once a Gropius sunrise in Nebraska
    smiling without hours
    delicately and green.

STORM

I felt the lightning go through me
    and waked.
Raining hard. Only night and flashes
    cracking, blasting,
        natural fact, natural beast,
            morality-vice,
    hacking and hopping —   one leg,
       three legs —   socking
          the single oak, socking
            the lake,
    fancy footwork cloud-to-cloud too fast to see,
       too bright not to see,
          cut through me

    then dropped me,
       shaking its fist spasmodically,
          backing away, away.

I lay shuddering,
    half hiding, half hopping.
I loved it.
It came.

NEXT YEAR

everything will be bigger:
six-inch growth on rhododendrons,
    green leather,   hide of embryo;
every pine a foot farther up the sky;
sweet woodruff,   sidling among bulbs
    as if unthoughtup

there will be more money:
no need to check the tag
    on nursery potlings;
I'll have the 10 ft. thorn
to bloom the first year,
    a tree before I'm old

I will know more:
the disillusion of camellia
    the afterthought of invasives
the reserved judgment of bone meal;
I'll be a black forest of folk wisdom
    floored with green cones

there will be more time:
my engagement book blank
    but for numerals,   sixteen, seventeen, eighteen;
no unscheduled absences,   the names of the months
in unhurried sequence:
    January is waiting,
the others are busy
uncalendrically,
    May for example is raking,
she's collecting brown leaves like moisture,
preparing a wayside
    where schemes may fall

the weather will be better: drought ending;
rain,   rain flying up from the SW
    will dangle blowing
against my loved porch
blowing in on the porch
    spattering the empty rocking chairs
swelling their dead wood
like embalming fluid

I won't miss the ducks' migration:
stepping into the night by my gate I'll hear
    the appointed skytramping,
the comradely call; who knows?
it may be my year to share
    the vacant eye full of destination

CASTING ABOUT

> "At Cross Creek Bill Long limited on bass Wed.
> A.M. using a purple floating worm."
> — CrossCreek Fish Camp

1

To limit on something! —
rocking in a boat
drifting in open water,
eyes glazed by the sun,
at "a sport where you don't keep score,"
they tell me,
"where experience itself is the object
of the game," they assure me,
though lure after lure is torn in shreds
by acres of ladyfish.

One who's never been out
fishing in the bonnets,
never caught 30 blues
within an hour — not even one —
never been finned by a sunshine bass,
I am re-reading the saved-up clippings:
Freshwater Outlook
Gulf Update
sitting by my window in the hinterland,
running with the dorsals and the pectorals
in Lochloosa.
Outside, a man on legs
drives a leaf-blower, ear-rending,
leaving a snuffy wake behind.

But Gainesville makes short shrift of winter —
> *On March 18 a crabber reported seeing*
> *a kingfish in the air in 17 ft. of water. . . .*
> *A caster reports the specks are in the trees.*

This new alluring world's still not my own.
I go into its darkness

as if I'm speeding on a train at night,
my berth shade raised,
and strange lights crashing by —
racing into secrets on ahead,
secrets fleeting, unaware I'm glimpsing them —
my own solution, like one's palm,
unfathomable to oneself.

Freshwater Outlook. Gulf Update.

Reports, bewildering as those sent back
to Spain, from farers to the Terra Neuva,
I puzzle at: "Today, off Ponce de Leon Inlet,
manta rays with their cobia garlands."
Those black ploughshares
with ears inturned on top — sea devils —
haunt the spring of innocence?

I puzzle at
Specks in the trees.
                In the cypresses
fishers propel their boat,
pulling by cypress knees
through dead gunmetal water.
Fishing in the bonnets?
                I find the entries:
"Spatterdock," "cowlily". . . .
    I took the bait under a lily pad. . . .
    The lily, the lily, the rose I lay. . . .
No clues from a line miscopied in a monastery.
So much for in-His-image accuracy.

        But there's a fine-tuned fish
        snubs water 74 degrees;
        he's set for 75.
        In Orange Lake the islets float;
        their trees, to 20 ft.,
        sail with the wind,
        and heron hens pursue their nests
        around the lake unruffled.

But how do fish get there?
How do they find these lakes
hollowed by rushing-in collapse,
the land hourglassing downward — land emptying
as water emptied from Payne's Sea
when nature pulled the plug,
stranding a little steamer
high and dry — flat-out mud-logged —
as the lake drained underground?

> The marsh creeps back
> upon Payne's Prairie now
> with water grass
> and trickling pools
> and fishing ibises.

In Northern Florida, a placid field,
a vacant lot, somebody's yard —
gasps suddenly, and earth pours down
until the sinkhole's deep enough
for creeklets to seek out
and make a lake of,
a lake fish somehow find.
How deep is it? I asked the agent.
Oh–*bottomless*, she swore, breathless.

> *It is reported Wednesday's sinkhole*
> *that opened at the Marion County ramp*
> *is not, as had been feared, draining the lake.*
> *Over the week-end specks bit well.*

2

Where is the catch I'm after, the bottom line?

> I set out, with my ammunition:
> red hackles, surface plugs —
> a tray of last-meal choices —
> bent not on food — dominion.
> *And the dread of you shall be*
> *upon the fishes of the sea.*

It's my right.
A licensed angler,
shall I work the oyster bars
for 7 trout, one mackerel?
>   Limit on specks, fishing
>   just over the hydrilla in 7 ft.?
or take, in the trees,
a nice mess of males
just starting fanning?

Or, invading the *sanctuaries*,
in Dame Juliana's name —
black hideouts in the cypresses — pull fish
from pools small as a convent table?

or fish near Homosasso Bombing Range? . . .
>   (*Enemy assuming helix pattern* —
>   *Take to brush shelter! . . .*
>   Which side am I on?

Which side should I be on?

Out of the sea
we lowly things evolved,
unequal and uncivilized.
Wherever there are two,
one is not free;
two species or two specimens.

>   Through my dazed bliss they move in, nibbling,
>   these questions of a lifetime,
>   on a lifetime — nibbling and gnawing.

I can't bypass the scales.
Between the bereaved simplicity of Cross Creek
and the deluxe of lodges in Montana,
I mean to weigh
that catch I'm after,
to tip these fishy scales.

We were all born lucky, said Hemingway, in Cuban waters.
And nine years later shot himself.

3

Suwanee River's sent
a discomposing note:
"A pigeon with bands on each leg
has set up station on the dock."
    A common pigeon.
    Not one of your outlandish
    grebes or frigate birds,
    or comic beggars at the bucket, pelicans.
Indictment's taken residence,
    shackles on both legs.
    Fishing in right, in law and order,
    killing for pleasure, or
    as we say, for knowledge,
    we spawn a code of wriggling questions.

I phobe myself into the fog
like heaven, or some Alaskan nowhere —
the fog that swept down over
Shirl Speight and Marge McGill
running them aground late-afternoon
in strange, hushed waters,
    where, in Treasure Trove's
    unsympathetic prose,
    they spent a cold night —
    and anxious morning
    till a Coast Guard copter
    caught their jacket-waving
    and they were led out
    by two boaters from the Key,
    not ravenous for scrambled eggs,
    but for the dock, their legs.

While Bill Long limited on bass, the lucky dog.

In Cow Creek I caught 20.
Small, but legal.
So he said.
> This king's domain, this paradise —
> shan't we serfs share it?
> Can't we control *his* rights?
Yet — when comunity's made king —
who'll dish out rights?
put shackles on my goings-out?
assess my surplus?
> Or — when I'm king — just me —
> I worked for it,
> I landed it, why should I
> go-frees with those pelicans?

Why do I spend
so many hours in futile casting?
Hours, I've spent,
fishing for conclusions
in schools of questions
out beyond my depth,
unfathomable, nibbling, gnawing —
fishing without a strike —
or throwing them all back.

4

Then I saw — a television rerun —
fishers on the grass flats in a little boat
haul in a sunshine bass, a legless spangle
battling to stick to water,
writhing like a bagged cat —
like Mr. Clutter when the cold-blood boys
savaged his son — as futile, too,
his stout mouth gaping like a kite for wind,
a drowning man for breath.

I stared.
They were killing him.
Fin them! Fin them! I begged the fish.

No, they threw him back —
a barb big as his heart inside his jaw,
or with a gash where flesh tore out.
Not murder — torture.
No matter, whether he remembered, next week —
whether he was a brave fish —
didn't *they* remember?
   Wait.
I like fish on the table, like anybody else.
I like law and order and property.
I, too, like turning the nightmare
out of the daylight of my life,
don't like accusers on the dock.
I mean to stay as silvery in the livewell
as nature will allow.

  To limit on something!
  Playing a deadly sport without opponents,
  I still want scorecards.

Or could I somehow,
drifting half in dream,
achieve two viewpoints in one space,
somehow accept one impasse in two runs —
letting experience wash over, wash over —
eyes half unseeing,
past wonder and enchantment,
past dominion —
near the bombing range, in shallow water,
on a peaceful mission?

If I could leave it at that!
     But why —
why, after all our education, our syllogisms,
our subsidies, our prayers, etc. —
why is the water stained,
our visibility muddied, not just
"offshore as far as Big Bend Marker 12"?

II

WILDERNESS OF LADIES

THE BINE YADKIN ROSE

Bemiracled rose, I see my cutting took:
Sad horn, the spell-rocked cradle of a rose —
Look! how the foster brier grows
That mother bed, that lover bed forsook.

Miss Tempe went to sew for Miss Bine
Before she ever thought of being Mamma,
The smoothing, the whistling, a scissorly-wise drama,
Her life a raggy scrapbag pantomime.
    (The artful rose of stiff, dispiteous stem
    Blenched lest a natural beauty should offend.)

Miss Bine taught one to violet the wrists.
"I accuse you, Mr. Stapleton,
Of excess temperance — ha-ha!"
"Miss Tempe. . . . I beg. . . . Allow me to insist — !"

In autumn near dusk a bad cloud came up.
The heavens turned drear, Miss Bine turned white.
"I fear God is near," she croaked. "Let's light a light."
They set a fiery candle in a teacup.
    (The spicy daughters of rank greenhouse whims
    Blench lest a natural vanity offend.)

Unringed, but wed, she took a ring and wed unwed,
A bouquet of pink hyacinths at her waist.
Her thumping heart denied her chilling taste
But well believed the deadly words she said.

Move into a house that's not yet built,
And there's scant time to prune a rose and spray.
You dish potatoes up three times a day,
And put your wedding dress into a quilt.
    (The chary husband stiff dispity wins
    Quails lest uxorial charity set in.)

Pray let me not unduly understand
This ring-a-rosy of our distant hands,

Nor color up, just barely cultivate;
An austere blossom for each Sunday plate,

For a sisterhood in multiple rosettes,
Adoring our Victorian regrets.

MOVED

No more carting in or out or off,
No more saying old or new; instead
We'll dust the smiles that are discovered:
All is distributed.
Today for the first time
Mrs. Presterling revised
A spontaneity; I dropped my eyes.

Last things close in upon us
Like storm windows hung a week too soon.
Between the mullions I stare out into
The placid incubator where
Other life, somehow, cares to move.

To this address they will come,
All the bad news of losses that must be.
To this we desolate will come,
Older, from our other homes.
And I know certainly now, come or not,
Our line-oak softened at the core with rot,
The woods grown deeper so that simple light
Falling across the path perplexes sight,
The houses frailer and an ell, a porch,
Drawn off in chains behind a tractor,
The tractor back to smooth the pitching hills,
Our garden hung with hardening gourds,
A spot where idle birds whet idle bills.

And Mrs. Presterling, sweet heartsbane still
But gone drawn white and pinched, at our back door
Holding a coat together at her throat
With long blue fingers; rapidly and loudly:
"My husband's fallen, and I think he's dead."
She does not know whether to hurry, or
To stop on the path by the pitcher bed.

And we will languish idly in the yard-chairs.
How strange the shadows of the chickens are!
Because the sun is changing at this time, my dear;
In an hour or so all will be dark.
And there will be the spot upon the table
Where you or I set our last medicine glass,
As if a clapperless glass bell
Were covered by another, were covered by another,
Covered by a larger, clear
Glass bell.
Will there not be liftings-up?
Will there not be lazy breakfasts, with friends?
Will there be births in spiraling gardens?
Yes yes, but this is of ends.

PLAYING

In Ugly Creek they dashed their toes.
The Cyril Mabry cows arose
And water spiders stepped aside
To watch how little girls would wade;
A summer picnic well delayed
Might miss the churn-turned fireside.

Those old folks always have been old . . .
Those childhoods tell-re-over-told
Are just a pocket full of seeds
That never generated weeds. . . .

When the little girls returned to the bank
Their little fingers swelled and shrank!
A frigid, leafless shadow lay
Upon the water-throated day.
They piled their hands to play a game —
Pretense had always been their aim. . . .
What was it, little girls became?
Take it off, knock it off, or
Have the crows peck it off — ?
The little hands . . . they somehow shake;
The little bones they somehow quake.

Where's my share? Cat got it.
Where's cat? In the woods.
Where's woods? Water squenched.
Where's ox? Rope lynched.
Where's rope? "Dead and buried
Behind the new church door
And the first that laughs or grins or shows
His teeth
Gets a slap, and a kick, and a knock, and a —
Wreath."

The female bitter black tongues hum
The palms forsake the stiffened thumb
(The waiting womb! the waiting tomb —
The empty antique sitting room!)
Before the final griefs succumb —

ROBERT, YOU LEFT OUT SOME!
You left out some!
You left out some!
Watt . . . left out some. . . .

WIND

From the moment Gabriella died
At an exhausted, nightless morning time
A knifestruck disattendance cast a gloom
In any place she might have chanced to be,
Even in places properly mine —
In my bedroom, at my fireside —
That made me rise at once and leave a room
Instantly her formal blank came in to me;
The one last-minute, dry-pen silence drew
A grave, regretful, canceling line through
All my blotted teas. There was nothing to say
And it was no use looking for anything,
In the cupboards, or out the door.
Long ago, something had eaten out my marrow,
And I was hungry now, for years before.

My flaxseed-meal aunts touched my arm:
"Faith holds no room for such alarm —"
But the wind of a suddenly-turned season,
Hard, and raw enough to move a solid shadow,
Began in flaws to rush the outer closures
And wheedle through the inner apertures,
Calling together broken flowered cups,
Uncommunicative inked-out reasons,
Recalling losses that had hinged
On cheese toast and the cats' piece-meals;
I even felt my cradle agonies
Alone, in the dark back room, revealed
In the wind fighting the oaks, seizing life
Just so. In the wind's seizure I saw her
Trudging barefoot and mudfouled
Over the clay with strength grown bodywise,
And wherever the dreamy, cultivated
Part of her had fled to —
It was not in her ghost, nervous, human eyes
I kept seeing.
                    Gabriella, howl!

SISTER

And we two alone here in this peace pan
Are ever strolling uphill to the old-house-place;
The path washed out, grown up, but not erased:
The wars of marriage and the family burst around us.

When I was young, folks thought me pretty.
I took my charms up to the city. . . .
I didn't like it there.
   Oh, the poems Mamma burned in those days!
You made Mamma cry. Her tears fell in the dough . . .
I'm not well, that's why. I told you so.
Why did you go and have me? I hate you all.
   Lord, help me to be more humble in this world.
(Don't tell on me. I hid the pieces in the dungeon.)
   Lord, help me to be more humble in this world!
   In that Great, Getting-up Morning, there will be another
      song!

In the old-house there was cotton,
Piled shoulder high to climb on,
Soundless and seedy — exotic,
And the floor smelled seasonround of guano.
We walked about and about the house at night.
Hear the frogs creak in the pasture! (I thought
The stars made that noise when they came out)
No! no! no! no! my dear!

Then we discovered within the close
Our exotic properties, our pretty price.
The garden radish lies on ice, the radish rose.
Smorgasbord! and the 'Venerable
Silver-throated horn' unsounded;
Dinner on the grounds! and the blessing still unsaid;
The sun that baked our mud-bread
Hides slyly in the trees
Between Spring Garden and Milton Streets
And howls at what we eat.

And riding the trolley homeward this afternoon
With the errands in my lap
I would have disfestooned my world —
A husband, more or less!
A family, more or less! —
To have alighted to a cup of kettle-tea
And someone
To whom I could lie merrily,
Use malapropisms, be out-of-taste,
Without regretting that old warfare waste,
Without acknowledging the sib discard —
Black king, black jack, black heart;
We'd play it solitary while the dusks rushed by,
More than one-flesh-and-blood,
Almost one I.

GOODBYE FAMILY

The sounds I hear from the evening chambers
    Stanch my breath.
Whether I sit alone in the parlor
    Or whether
Ladies crack nuts and ice cubes there, I hear
    Tiptoeing,
A banging head, and breath stops for fear
    Of what I am doing there
Clanging and pacing in the rooms
    Of next year.
For hate-you paralyzed my lover's shrug;
    My stare
Froze down the only warmth another had,
    All her own;
Each year I dug and moved the peonies
    Longing to flare
Fat and chemically by the well-slab,
    Ingrown.
Every day I opened the drawer and
    Scanned the knives;
Were there enough, sharp enough,
    For all lives?

The years to climb! The walls to catch at!
    To cut free
And drop through the cloak closet and cellar
    Is better —
Under the foundations of God's world
    Lilily
Swimming on my side, with ear on shoulder,
    Eyes unlettered,
And intellectuality an asterisk
    Now blurred —

It's no use God's whistling, "Come back, Fido,
    "Come back,
"I won't tease any more." I'm in the glade
    Remembering
I meant to tell my daughter, "I looked for
    You a cattail
But they were all silked out" —
    And now the water
Meeting me around the curve, roaring, blanks
    Out all but ear:
        Not in the day time, not in the dark time
        Will my voice cut and my poison puff
        My treasures of flesh
        My gems of flashing translucent spirit,
        Nor my caress shatter them.

BUCK DUKE AND MAMMA

He came bringing us a milkpail full
Of speckled, wild, goose plums —
All fat unsmelt-out perfumedom —
And perched on the back porch curb to taste a few
"Sour! Your eyes'll water, Miss Tempe!
But sweet, too."
Mamma's way was posing by the silent pool
And tossing in the line amiss
That shook the skies of the other world
And all but loosed the roots of this.
She trimmed and trained the roundabout backwoods,
Was glad that Buck Duke had a devilish eye;
It saved an orphan from dire fortitude,
And saved his grandpa's house from sanctity.
"Your Papa doesn't favor your going there.
I say, enter evil to cure evil, if you dare!"
As she went about her cast-off household chores
She overlooked them with a lavish bow
Inspired by that heroine of poems,
Her elocution teacher, Miss Hattie Yow.
        "Nothing to do? In this world of ours?
        Where weeds spring daily amidst sweet flowers?"
        Your-mammy-never-came-to-much-my-Buck.

"Don't drink that Mackling Spring's brack water
Whe'r it's high or low.
The cows stand in there and let go."
But old Duke's beardy words were moss for campfire
When they took their kitchen rations to the woods.
Mamma's boys looked out for sassafras, but Buck
Made frog gigs, thrashed Mackling Spring into a suds.

("I say, dear boys! Be good. Take care.
But learn a little evil! if you dare. . . .")
His thirst once drunk, turned drunken,
And Buck Duke tossed all night, all day,
Made rusty speeches on old swapping knives,
Called names that paled the sallow-boned herbwives,
Tore off the sleeping clothes, his bed's, his own,
And never seemed to wake.
His boyish modesty ran dry,
At last the hands cooled, then the face.
Mamma stood at his bedside.
She overlooked him with a sprightly brow
Inspired by that gay mistress of mad poesy
Her elocution teacher, Miss Hattie Yow.

    " 'Stop stop pretty waters' cried Mary one day
    'My vessel, my flowers you carry away.' "

Mamma made a wreath of all her flowers:
The histrionic garden did not bear
One saucy pose when she put down the scissors;
The battered bees hung stupid in mid-air.
She worked on knees and elbows on the back porch,
That savage zinnia ornament compiled,
Then all at once cooped up her face
With hands like bird's wings —
A gesture, she knew, would have made Miss Hattie smile.

COUSIN IDA

She waked to snow,
And let the morning go,
For she was old.

That hushed onset
Comes but to blank
My distant, might-be-yet world, too,
All worlds, all peep shows in all eggs.

On the piazza, from east edge sunburnt
To west edge burnt, our voiles still warm
From the iron, we rocked, our passage learnt,
Hemstitching and featherstitching, charmed
Yet sighing, that heat and light went hand in glove.
We prepared for marriage, or — rather — love.

One night he'd had a drop too much (my beau
Smiled gently but was not a gentleman)
Snored by the parlor fire and scorched his toe.
They found that highly entertaining.
But while I was gone off to Beulah Springs
They cut my wedding dress to jabots
And I came back without a ring or hope.
(How droll of me to love a parlor joke!)

Flora, Ida, Tempe — Tempe wryly
The day black Uncle Wylie died:
"Good-bye-sir, Wylie!
"You ought t've been gone from here long ago!"
We took him figs and tea a year;
He kept his shoulder to the wheel of death.
We never combed our hair ourselves
Till we were twenty, and Tempe said,
"It tires one so, combing one's hair;
"I give out in my shoulders;
"Let's do each other's now."
But Ida rising from her vanity —
"Not I! We should've been gone from here long ago."

About my shoulders now the snow
That was a fall of stars. . . .
>When the stars fell it was unearthly bright;
>We read unwritten texts by that sharp light.
>"More rain, more rest —"
>>"What's that you say?"
>"Master, more rain, more grass!"
>World's coming to an end.
>And Guinea, that's gone, too,
>Cold sparks just out of reach.
Afterwards, the night was dark; wind rose,
A smoky wind, and I waked
Listening, twice towards dawn,
To see if the world went on.

Does this hushed onset come to blank
My distant, might-be-yet world, too?

I, captive, cage-fond,
Dread doors opening on the great beyond.
That bird they said had no song of her own
Cries from the black gum to my ears alone
The very sentence she would say when I was four.
You leave me untranslated, wife of snow!
But now it's grown midnight.
Don't scream for glossaries.
Sh, bird. Let's sleep.
Within our feathered wings,
Within our snow.

One year I clapped my hand over my eyes
When spring came, and when I took it down
My knuckles were speckled brown.
In the middles, in the red cotton bloom,
Each warm clod with its darker side,
Its sprouting seeds of the staved-off jungle,
Slaves still sang:
Tiding down the backband, tiding down the bow
Tiding down the backband, who made the bow?

Not I! Good-bye-sir-Wylie!
We should've been gone from here long ago!
God made the bow.

They bound me up in ribbons, moiré bows,
My hair so tight it left no play for face,
My waist so tight it left no space for plea.
"Child, you'll be miserable," they warned, "Don't go."
(Stay here where suffering's homemade, sure to fit.)
Mine never has worn out, though it's grown thin
Now, like a veil. I see through it
When the shadows are right. Light dwindles
In the outer world, and my own ember,
Knocked about like a goody in a nut,
Shines smally through — dormant — convoluted —
Half a notion to spill out.
The deaths of my sisters seems known
To me already; soon, my own;
Chill comes and goes; warm life's phenomenon.
I find myself waking in the night,
Listening to see if the world goes on.
My quick, half-lighted shower, are you gone?

THE CHAIN GANG GUARD

The pick strikes differently on the rock
And some resists and some dislodges.
The cars that pass us eye us curiously —
Stodged with our eyes, our frozen triggers cocked.
They move free enough; for them, they're jolly —
The blond one, swinging, sings, "Just like a tree,
Just like a tree, planted by the waters,
I shall not be moved." Easy to see
His spirit's not yet broken. That first chow —
Nose took a squint and stomach shut its eyes;
"I can't eat that," he said. The others spat.
"You may think you can't, but, brother, you lie!"

I don't dare glance to hail the folks I know.
He'll curse or laugh or both as he sees fit,
Cry out to give a stranger's ears a whack,
And throw his hat up for a powdered nose,
Baby oh baby oh baby her,
Die to know where she's off-to up the road.
Playmate, you aint going nowheres
Unless you want to hear my gun unload.

If I had ever learned to tear-up-jack,
Got drunk enough to leave myself behind,
Could know which time to take and which to pay —
Here I stand! loaded gun across me —
As if I'd get away!

IN THE CHURCHYARD

In the churchyard I hear them hammering
On the new roof of my new house
A hundred years old.
Cupped acorns glut the walks,
The greenish nuts crushed in.
Cupped earths hold up the bright memorial ferns.
They're gone!
Down over Mamma's face
They nailed, we nailed, I nailed the lid.
And there was Uncle Risdon.
Married a Miss Catherine Tye. Aunt Catherine
Somehow I can't now call her full name.
She took a galloping consumption
After she let the baby catch on fire.
Aunt Oratha despised the coat
That Uncle bought her. She died of pride.
Pride knoweth neither hot nor cold
But hers knew both.
They die of fleshly pride.
And Cousin Mazeppa took laudanum.
"Why did you do it, Zeppie, girl?
Wa'n't Daddy good to you?"
"Pray, let me sleep!"

Child, brave it to blind-out the fur
Of the evergreens in sun above:
They are too far;
Shade has rinsed out their sun,
Hushed up their green.
They'll dizzy one.

There's the rattat of the hammers —
The little nails, the little nails,
The birds eat out one's hands!

NIGHT

I spent the night in Chastelton.
The splitting damasks hung in belts;
Those faded colors we admired
Forgot themselves in gray.
Light spider-bagged the baseboards, tired.
I climbed up to the children's room.
I knew the way.
Up steps and past a blistered stile
Along that thick oak balustrade
(You like old things? Behold!)

The carved door hung ajar.
I pushed it wide.
The birds flew from their roosts
And disappeared like mice into the sky.
Below, the garden that one time
Held itself clipped urns, hens, cones,
Of evergreen, had turned
A calendar of wastes,
A zodiac of despairs.
There was somebody there.

It was you.
You were a mortal sheen
Flickering from the negative.
You were younger than last year,
Younger than the day we were married,
Younger than the day we met.
What are you doing?
To whom are you smiling?
Where are you going?
Will you not answer me?
Answer! Answer!

WOMAN AS ARTIST

I'm mother.
I hunt alone.
There is no bone
Too dry for me, mother,
Or too extra.

Have a care, boy.
The neat pearls nibbling at the chowder
Gently, with joy,
Contain powder.

    An emigrant from the mother tongue
    To say-so in the silent one,
    For me the stepped-for step sinks,
    The expected light winks
    Out; dear self, do not think
    On the ominous appetite rising insistently
    In the hour of no food. . . .
    Do not think of the mice in the clock
    When you start up in your sleeping hood.
    The light feathers of a year,
    Too fine to make a pillow,
    Not fine enough to wear
    Out anywhere, drop but like milk
    Into the snow
    Of what I say and bear.

Kneel, fathers.
If my babies are right,
It is not because of you!
Or me.
But I lick them dearly,
Scrutinize their toilette,
Every tendril pleasing
On account of me. . . .

Next year I'll dig them up
And separate them.
They'll multiply
    Multiply
        Multiply
Till the round earth's ringed with Babel trumpets,
Some dark, some light,
Some streakèdy.

When I first gave the question life,
The howling naked question life,
Did I not have some inkling of the answer,
And the answer answered,
The door that closed across the room
As my door opened?

    In the morning, early,
    Birds flew over the stable,
    The morning glories ringed the flapping corn
    With Saturn faces for the surly light,
    And stars hung on the elder night.

    But in the afternoon
    Clouds came
    Cyclonic gusts and chilling rain
    Banged-to the windows of our heroine
    Beginning to chronicle her wound-up skein.
    Rib, spin.

ROMANTIC ABSTRACT

Believe in me,
Who always meant to be.
I never can.
         (I'm told
She slaps the baby's dirty hands,
The dishes mold.)

We were always apart in the dark
In deck chairs, shaking our heads
In vexation at our questions.
The light-tongued stars that spat the flower bed!
The mute, placed moon that stood stock dead!
The doctor would diagnose his soul:
Unreal, so, functional, he holds.

Does it matter whether it unlives at Anzio
Saving lives (mostly undertaking)
Or rotting as a yeasty testy case
(It nettled me to have them touch my dog
And say in their dispelling voices, *Dog*)
Or when the wifely salad hits your face?
                      (They tell me
She'll be found tippling
In the bright lonely rooms;
The receiver swings,
According to the laws of pendulums.)

You should have struck a light
In the dark I was, and
Said, Read, Be — be over!

We should have been leaning
Together over the window sill
Upstairs, watching the Milk Dipper
When the building fell.

That stricture in the upstairs throats
Would have been indeed the proper note.

But now no longer I, I will be she —
The one who didn't wait, but always does,
Who haunts your sickbed, fever-yearned:
She-just-she will hold her hand
Over the wound as you turn.

OUT OF HABIT

Plague take the way I call to mind
Things out of habit!
Cousin Risdon comes and sits
Against the window,
(I'd fear to see me better,
But he went blind at Argonne)
Refuses anything to drink,
(So I could fly out to the kitchen
For a minute, cry alone)
Puts his black bag at his feet
(Though actually he never reached med school —
That little pretense is so sweet).
I cry anyway, on my charm bracelet:
We were just the same age;
If I hadn't been a girl
I might have gone too. . . . Yes yes
I will dry up.
You don't mind if *I* smoke?
Remember reading Hambone in the swing?

But he desires to parley in black leather.
    Susan,
    The human eye is a wonderful thing.
    Through the lid, through sleep,
    We perceive day and wake.
    The eye accustoms itself to darkness,
    To delicate variations.
    After a number of years of darkness
    One might, suddenly, as seeds perceive,
    Perceive the light, sifting like rainfall,
    Like the sun drawing water,
    Through the porous earth
    To our soft coffins —
    For light does penetrate
    Cloud, night,
    Lids, sleep,
    Earth —
    Why not death?

SONG

Oh my dearie,
Our childhoods are histories,
Buckets at the bottom of the well,
And hard to tell
Whether they will hold water or no.
Did Pa die before we were married?
No, he died in twenty-seven,
But I remember the wedding
Reminded me of the funeral —
When the grandbabies ask,
Little do they care,
I will tell them about the man I found
That day at my plowing in the low-grounds
Lying at the edge of the water.
His face had bathed five nights.
A dark man, a foreigner, like.
They never found his kin to tell. . . .
Buckets, buckets at the bottom of the well.
It was in the paper with my name.
I found him.
I have the clipping tells all about it,
If your Grandma aint thrown it out.

Oh my dearie
When our faces are swol up
We will look strange to them.
Nobody, looking out the door
Will think to call us in.
They'll snap their fingers trying
To recollect our names.
Five nights, five bones, five buckets —
Who'll ever hear a sound?
Oh my dearie
The rope broke
The bucket bobs round
Oh my dearie

MY GRANDMOTHER'S VIRGINHOOD, 1870

When I disrobed to go to bed
It seemed to me like something said:
Hold your shimmy round you tight —
Somebody may be around tonight —
Aint no curtain, aint no shade —
Don't hurt none to be afraid —
    Little David McSwain!

Walked us both home from the dance
Wearing new black homespun pants.
When we got up to the door
Catched us both around the waist
And — kissed us! Lor!
What's he getting — kisses! from us for?
    Little David McSwain!

MOTHERHOOD, 1880

When Dave got up and struck a light
We'd neither of us slept all night.
We kept the fire and watched by May,
Sick for fear she might
Go off like little Tom. . . . They say
"Don't fret . . . another on the way. . . ."
They know I favor this least child.

No use to cry. But while
I made a fire in the kitchen stove
I heard a pesky mourning dove.
Lor! What's he calling "O-love" for?

FAMILY BIBLE

1. Uncle

Typical of the presents
Grandma gave Grandpa
Was Uncle Mun,
A baroque buckle
Not to be undone.
He thought before he spoke,
Abstained from drink, snuff, smoke,
Marriage; ate and dressed frugally,
Reproved respectfully
His mother's yen
For jet beads on her birthday.
Was it not thoughtful of him
On her busy death day
As she counted quilt-blocks
To elicit this data
In Spencerian pencil
Laid away in the clock
For me,
Posterity?
 My full name is Aminta Dunlap Watkins Ross.
 My mother was Merina Wilkerson.
 My father was Arnold Watkins — he carpentered —
 I married your pa Whitson Ross
 My wedding presents were a feather bed and two hens.

2. Grandmother

The hens gone on the honeymooning coach,
Squawking and scratching at the black hope chest;
She made her bed and it was hard, for rest
Too hard; when broken dreams and sleep encroached
Upon stark wakefulness, she walked the stars;
Her unread eye imagined what they meant:

Job's Coffin and the Seven Sisters, the fine-print
Groups; then what said those blazing sky-far,
A sky not like a page, a script not like a word,
But taking or leaving a star,
A world, as it just chose?
How the hymn book puzzled her,
Singing "Jesus and Shall" —
And the notes of the music,
If one read, like the choir!
'Tis midnight in my soul till He
Bright morning Star! bid darkness flee.

3. Grandfather

The fear of hell was all,
His children wheezed,
That wore Whit Ross's pants
Out at the knees.
His poverty enraged him
(A hoe
To cultivate flint rocks,
Breeches to thwart the briers)
His wits fanned up his ignorance
Like a fire.
Something savage in him
Fought civility.
If he had but been born nobility!
Beaten sexless lifeless
Souls touched him.
When a black boy Joe died —
What had he ever had
From life to give to death?
He found a far-off part
Of meadow land
To cry his tears.
"A Christian spirit needs
Not cherry bounce,
Mint, be a good woman —
The Bible says!"

4. Grandparents

The Bible says!
The Bible looked not right to her.
It should be short, straight rules,
Not run-on continuities the stops left out
So hard to read for true.
The Bible says!
She wept before the finger.
She sought out her eldest son
In the middle of the day.
"Boy, pray for me."
His coattails, her calico black skirts
Puddled about the shoes and knees.
Was it forgiven? It was gone,
The heathen dancing
With her giggling sisters;
They flew about the room
In seedstitch weskits
Like eight wax dolls gone flaskwards.
Those were gay days!
She sighed a mournful tune
Waddling about her everyday
Affairs of life and death
(Affairs of painful life, uncertain death):
"Wild loneliness that beats
Its wings on life," she sang.
She thwacked a pone in two,
Her big hand for a knife.
Thar! stirring it severely,
And thar! into the oven . . .
'Twould be wormwood and ashes.
A spray of peacock feathers
Begged from her father's house
Splattered the dining room wall.
(She pretended to Whit
That she dusted with it.)
The table was small for nine;
The honeycomb, buttered,
Hived in glass vines.

5. Granddaughter

When she was old, deaf, widowed, my grandmother,
She came to spend a lonely night at home.
When I went to call her in to breakfast
She did not hear my brave voice for her comb
Running through her hair in little flights —
(Long, long hair as much gold as white,
Flying with old-fashioned electricity
From the comb's old-fashioned friction)
And as she rocked, her shell-combs on her knee,
Suddenly aware, she looked up at me
Through her shimmering hair, startled, and smiled.
Air ye awake, little gal?
Perhaps she thought I was admiring her.
She gave a proud, delighted, sidewise smile
Flashing her small gray teeth and elf-arched eyes,
For a ninety-eight-point-six degrees' response.
But she was disappointed, though I smiled.
Her silent island threatened me enchantment;
The joints too lithe to creak when I bent over
Sailed off without retrieving for her
A big bone hairpin wrecked upon the floor.

The day she was buried
I played sick and lay abed
Claiming fever.
I did not see her dead.
But eight months before
At Rehobath Church
On Homecoming Day
I stood with a crowd
Of boys and girls, and
Watched her cross the churchyard
Slowly, alone; from end to end
She crossed the yard,
Her head thrown back,
Swathed deep in black —

Long skirts, pointed black toes,
The wind parting her many veils,
The blue eyes beneath roving, veiled —
And leaning on a stick.
She seemed a giant Figure,
All eyes upon her;
Yet none spoke.
And all my heart said,
Run to her! Claim her!
(Wild loneliness that
Beats its wings on death)
Then the spell broke.
We who had waved across so many chasms
No longer had to say we were not close.
Was closeness more than painful separateness?
We were a constellation of detached, like, ghosts.

III

WELCOME EUMENIDES

CHAPTER AND TEXT

Brother, we must converse somehow.
Given but the hour,
Juxtaposed thus,
It seems only human.
Yet how to key your tongue
So like the hieroglyphics of your stare,
A seam, a clef, a stamen —
How wreak on silence your mute voice,
How smoke your blind face from the asterisks?
I fear you, stabbed dragon.
I understand the snarl, born of the word.
I pity you, winged jackass in the leaves.
Oh, I despair of myself
That your Berlitz is too simple for me.
    Yet, when you lie across the bed,
Eyes shouting at the ceiling,
Hand clenching letters out of all syntax —
I see what you mean.
Our language exists but in silence. . . .
Our mortality in immortality.

AFTER TWENTY YEARS

After twenty years in France
Do you dream in French, my son? . . .
Home . . . ça existe encore.
Still, still exists Flagg Bros. store,
With new glass front, but behind
The dilapidated sheds
And packed road lined with maypops
Where you talked to the white horse.

Gloved, hatted, I kneel here
Where you by the sky-blue windows
Sang "Onward Christian Soldiers."
For I have needed pardon
Since the morning we found Dad
In the garage (It is hard
To be a father without
A son). I screamed, and without
A son to be a widow.
Shall I pray your pardon too?
Prince of Peace, absolve all warriors,
My warrior of the bow and arrow.
Your old girl married money.
She's grown stout. (*He* has ulcers.)

Last year they were in Nice
Not Normandy. . . .
My glove's rouge, with lipstick
Or with teeth. . . . Curse *men*, curse *free* —
God vault your freedom!

Oh the acres of undistinguished
Crosses make me sick.
Mother could mark Papa's grave
In the churchyard a mile from home,
By its firs and shaft. . . .
Your nothing grave . . .

Shame!
God I am of little understanding. . . .
But with God all things are possible. . . .
Give my son another life —
A Norwood ugliness, a bourgeois rot,
Dust and concrete, Falcons and Mustangs, not . . .

THE GUARD REMEMBERS

Only a scullery maid
Running through the garden, sire,
Shoes in hand, cheeks white, her eye
Glittering as an hourglass. . . .

Time flies. . . .
At court the accent nowadays
Is countrified. Law speaks
In some magic of the king's bride:
In each oppressed face he meets
The imperial blue eyes by his side.

WELCOME EUMENIDES

> *"God called me in the morning and asked*
> *me would I do good for Him, for Him*
> *alone without the reputation."*
>
> F.N. March 7, 1850

Who calls?
Speak, for thy servant heareth. . . .

Is it the wards at Scutari?
Or the corridors at Waverly,
Where last night eighty slept.
Our masks — my pink gown with black lace —
Moving, at five, exhilarated,
Weary from dancing, up the famous stairs. . . .

    Mother! Nurse! water! . . .
    I come!

But now at five they have not slept
Except the men, heads blanketed, who crept
To timeless shadow.
Two thousand deathbeds that one winter.
Last May my window gave
On a thousand Turkish flowers,
Two thousand English graves.
Two thousand deathbeds that one winter —
    Who thinks of that now?

    Who calls?
Not my child
(*O God no more love*
No more marriage)
    Only my British Army.

(Dear Aunt Mai, kiss all babies for me.)
    Oh my poor men I am a bad mother
    To come home and leave you to your Crimean graves.
    73 percent in 8 regiments in 6 months
    From disease alone. (Who thinks of that now?)

There was a white rose in the New Garden cloister.
(The idol of the man I adored)
Richard, the sea breaks against the sea wall.
("You could undertake that,
When you could not undertake me.")
The plough goes over the soul.
    My Hilary ateliered,
    Femme espaliered, or, woman staked.
    The apricot bears against the south wall
    Daughters too basked at hearth.
    (No more love, no more marriage!)
Which of the chosen ever chose her state?
To hide in love!
Lord, seek Thy servant elsewhere. . . .
    Yet He calls.

I was not invited.
At home at Embly, Wilton, Waverly,
I, sated with invitations,
I, presented to the poor Queen,
I, worthy of the Deaconesses of Kaiserswerth,
Asked by the birthday child to every fête,

I was unwelcome.
The others came.
Two hundred by the shipload,
Jolted from stretchers,
Feverishly crawling up the hill
Through the ice-needled puddles.

I guarded the anteroom
Holding my nurses back, immune
To the cries, the sudden retching spasms, the all
But visible odors. (*Abandon hope all ye who enter here.*)
The mold grew on the walls.

[130]

Blessed are the merciful,
Says my crowned cross.

Pails of arrowroot, some port . . .
And then, all Balaclava broke loose.
Quick now, old sheets (the dying wait)
Speed, needle! This is no hooped French knot;
A deathbed is required.
    (Where did I yawn
    In the face of the gilt clock
    Defying it to reach 10?)
    Stuff straw for deathbeds, for deathbeds,
    For deathbeds.
    Not one shall die alone.
    I die with each.
    Now hurry to the next lax hand, loose tongue,
    Quick messages for forever.
    Mr. Osborne knelt down for dictation.
    His pencil skirmished among lice.
    At last, the chance for a rich and true life.

Outside, the wind rises.
    Wood! the fire dies. . . .
        There is no wood.
    The operating table then. Yes, chop it up.
        (For the operation Mr. Osborne
        Held up the patient with his arms and knee.)

Pen — paper — *vite!*
They demand supplies . . .
Ah ohhh the engine in my head. . . .
Claret and white flour for the Persian adventurer!
    Must I repeat:
Do not
    attach to the cutlets
    (1) rags (2) nails (3) buttons
    . . . surgical scissors

... that you can join me on the twenty-seventh
(Crème Harlequin aux Meringues — or dariolettes?)

And again. Please keep:
    a. Toilets covered.
    b. Windows open.
Orderlies: Eat not the rations of those men asleep.
    (*The éclat of this adventure of mine!*)

I dreamed . . .
Compulsive dreaming of the victim.
The rich play in God's garden.
Can they be forgiven?
Their errors gambol scintillating
Under the chandeliers like razors honed.
I murder their heaven,
I, starving, desperate, diseased. . . .
    ("You'll catch something and bring it home.")
Mother, you were willing enough
To part with me to marriage.
No, I must take some things;
They will not be given.
I dream.
    Saints are non-conformists,
    Ladies gone into service,
    Serving ladies with one talent;
    Cast ye the unprofitable servant into outer darkness.

Still-room, pantry, linen room.
Green lists, brown lists, red lists.
Come to me, yearbk of statistics
Of the Deaconesses of Kaiserswerth,
My love, my escape,
My share.
I dreamed of you; now I dream on you:
A hundred baby prayers;
All days garlanded with birthdays, prayers and flowers,
Rye tea. Elevenses: broth without bread:
At last, the chance for a rich and true life.

A girl, desperately fortified in my castle,
The starched pure linen,
Scalded plates, the sanitary air,
The facile word killed soul-ferment.
Six courses starved the spirit.
And I said of laughter, mad,
And of mirth, what is it doing?
I dreamed of all things at man's mercy.

Another boy reached for my hand.

Nurse, keep away. I'm filthy.
My own mother could not touch me.
And I looked sharply down. I was *not*
Wearing my great Paree panjandrum of black velvet.
It was my shawl, my pockets.
(It is not lady's work.)
I got the burned wing ready.
For eight hundred, sheets and warm food.
"I think I am in heaven," one soldier said.

Bridget looked up. A lady in black
Walked up the Lea Hurst drive.
Miss Flo! our little beauty —
Come home to die?
Or come home dead.
I have looked on Hell.

I wear black for you O British Army.

At night they flare in this soft room:
The long flickering wards,
The muddy uniforms, and sullied faces,
The black, dried, inky blood.
I can never forget.
I stand at the altar of the murdered men
And while I live I fight their cause.

Which of the chosen ever chose her state?
I who looked for some small stanch
Found the world's blood,
Armed with my handkerchief.
Armed with statistics:
Halt! wagons of the heavy artillery.
Cease and desist, wheels of the War Office.
    ("She wept very much.")
I survive them all.
I am sure I did not mean to . . .
No one ever did give up so much to live
Who longed so much to die.
Venez me consoler de n'être pas morte. . . .

. . . Much obliged, Dear George
For your Latin Hey Diddle Diddle
(O God no more love no more marriage.)

Ni lire, ni écrire, ni réfléchir.
I wear black for you O British Army.

    Another boy reached for my hand. . . .

Sir George, thank you
For the Greek Humpty Dumpty.
    (Still He calls.)
Venez me consoler de n'être pas morte.
Venez chez moi on Harley Street.
Bordure de jambon à la Sauvaroff —
Or . . . *quenelles de veau à la Villeroi?*
— The pungent meat pots at Scutari
Seasoned with iron pins, bolts, rusty nails
Tied to each packet.
A skinned sheep lay in the ward all night
To tempt our appetites.

The backed-up drains,
The floor inch-deep in sewage
Seeping under the door.
A thousand diarrheas vs. twenty chamber pots.
Ma'am, I've gone here.

Entry: March 10, 1866. *O!*

    I who could not live
    Without silence and solitude
    Harassed by Parthe's crewel Jesse tree . . .
    (Mother *lied* about the money). . . .
They left my owl locked in the empty house.
In my torment come dreams,
Dreams of Athena who left the Parthenon
To keep house in my pocket,
Forsaken in her feathers,
Her head winding and unwinding,
Eyes blank of me. . . .
Eyes at Scutari following
From cot, from floor, from table, winding-sheet.
For all things at our mercy
Give us grace.

WE ARE THE FRUIT

Tree-in-the-ground
And underneath, a lemon.
The lemon flies the tree,
Has no regrets.
Release is life.

Tree mourns
    It no more needs my thorns
    Flesh of my flesh
    Image of my image
    I cannot follow

Seed flutters
    Let me travel
    Ripening, ripening
    Reflecting the sun
    I know not the tree
    I know not the tree

But anchor to anchor,
Earth to earth, inside you yet
In the garden to come, lemon
Lie your own roots.

THE SKIPPED PAGE

If she stayed on her knees long enough
Maybe somebody would tell her
What she was doing in this house
So long unvisited;
What the beds were doing, made,
That had so long untidily held *them*;
What the sunlight did
Belaying the grimy pane;
And who was that, out there,
Sitting on a child's chair
Near the woodpile, holding a cane,
Facing the winter clouds
With fake fearless gilded eyes.

And she debated, turning her rings,
The dead telephone,
And how she would answer it there,
There where the knife was already in tomorrow
And her plate crying to receive the carcass.

TO A YOUNG WRITER

If you like love and fame
Shop early, get your shots
Don't spit, and pass with care —
Avoid at all costs
Death, breakdown, despair;
They'll fall on you,
Flock-peck to pieces wounded mouse:
I always thought so —
You know he lacked the drive
It had to come —
Dear friends consign you
To sanitorium, prison, and the pall.
No, keep your chair,
Tuck your wits in,
Say finally
I did outdure them all

THE YOUNG WRITER'S REPLY

But, sir, you know I saw the cops
Remove you from that Bleecker garbage can
Agog with pot.
Remember — analyzing Donne's Sermons
On your Payne Whitney cot?
(Your comments were brilliant, brilliant—
As noted in my journal on the spot.)
All of us heard you rake your wife
For coolness to your whore.
    We wrote it down.
        Laurel becomes a devastated brow.

COURTESY CALL, 1967

I'm back.

But you sleep now,
Who used to be the guardian of the stream.
It needs no guarding now; it's dreaming, too —
Narrower, deeper, sluggish, frosted with leaves.
I think it's comatose.
One used to see, a mile away, wind whip
Your leaves to wrongsideout to sun.
A wind could hardly find this glen today.
That hill was open pasture!
Just now I had to fight my way
To find a spot pine trunks
Were not too logjammed to squeeze through.
It was hard even to find you.
I thought I knew so well.
When the boys dug the swimming hole
They turned the stream;
But it's gone back now,
Their pool washed in,
Their turn filled in with trees —
Trees old (but younger
For trees than they are for boys) . . . .

Except that you've grown truly ancient . . .
I? The same.
The same, and elderly.
Like you trapped in some far neglect;
Reflections deepened, dulled,
Our voices out.

VICTORY

Granny Hill — no kin of course — said only sayings:
"Bad luck to drop your comb! Wind-storms come west . . .
"Bad luck to plant a cedar . . . it'll shade your grave."
Something forgotten, her face became obsessed;
She drew a cross-mark in her tracks,
Spat in the cross, before she would turn back.

The Saint girls mimicked her: Bad luck, bad luck!
"Come spend-the-night, girls—We'll eat boiled-butter-and-eggs."
Doctor Will, with a lantern, one fall night
Walked her orchard on dead legs,
And after that she had his power,
A remedy (some, though, severe)
For ingrown nails, chapped hands, consumption;
She talked fire from a swollen hand;
Was never sick herself.
Her face resided in a puckered bonnet;
Her clothes grew on her like a turtle's shell;
Bonnet and skirts smelled faintly henhouse.

Her Sally was a goose,
Shrill and dried up,
And where her baby came from no one knew
Unless it was George Jeans
Who drove the thresh.
But there was harmless Foolish John,
A man's beard, round black hat,
Round stomach like a two-year-old.
The Saint girls ran from him,
His grinning stare, the way he followed them.
He tore things up — old belts, old hats.
An old suspender was his favorite toy.
A moldy shoe found in the gully — Save it for John.

It was excitement,
Like George Jeans, the thresh, and chicken pie —
Three things he stabbed at saying,
Big-eyed, a prophet:
Geor' Jeans! Tresh? Chick' pie!

The Saint girls mimicked him,
Sometimes felt mimicked at the meeting house:
The turtleshell could say the Lord's Prayer backwards:
John sometimes said his words out loud,
Laughed, started for the pulpit.
A little screech from Sally brought him back.
"Whipping's all makes him learn," she'd wail.
They never saw him whipped or misbehave
(But taking off his clothes: "Like a baby —
Don't know no better.")

But one time he was lost three solid days.
Old Mr. Saint went out with them to search.
John! John-n-n!
They scoured the fields and woods all night
Carrying pine torches, calling,
(A lost dog would have come to whistling)
Stopping to stamp out broomstraw caught by sparks.
Three days, and gave him up.
Then found him under David Lee's cow-bridge,
Hovered, teeth chattering,
And led him home across the frozen fields.

Sunday he sat as empty as before.
Lord, whence are Thy hands so rent and torn?
They are pierc'd tonight by many a thorn!
Sally's high voice threw flames on the hymn;
The torches lit up Foolish John's pale face,
So much like hers, like Granny's — a pack of Hills —
And none of the ransom'd ever knew
How deep were the waters crossed
Or how dark the night the Lord passed through
Ere He found His sheep that was lost. . . .

John died first, of bloody flux;
Then Sally caught typhoid.
One morning Granny failed to wake.
Not dead, dried up and blown away, they thought.
Within a month Bess Saint at twilight
Appropriated Granny's shawl and bonnet,
Crept down from Granny's path to where the rest
Were picking berries. They threw their vessels
Far and wide, and to this day say, breathless,
"Bess, know that time — you dressed up like Granny?"

IRONWEED

In poverty of soil,
   in death of summer,
      I bloom —
         decree to bloom —
And in the color of kings.

SIRENS

They trail all travels.
Above the turbo-
Jet: the sirens' wail,
The ambulance
Arriving for one
I never expected
To leave. Below my bunk
Through hull a yard wide
In the land
Of phosphorescence,
Sirens; the attendant
Opens the white door.
Alien country,
Unpacked hotel —
Under the placid
Running bath, sirens,
Expectedly, sirens
Whispering for me.
(She died of internal
Weeping.)
Indestructible
Ears, have mercy.
Siamese partner,
If your heart fail
Shall I not panic?
Sirens have mercy
On my appendaged
Weeping
Lest I dissect us
With one nap.

ONE NOT DESCENDED

One not descended
From anybody
To those descended
From Mountbattens:

Arise, take hope.
Be queens
Of ascendancy.

Let those in ascendancy
Have dominion
Over those in descendancy.
Ascend, descendants.

O lowly descendants —
Mighty ascendants —

Bury the ladder and scend no more.

FLIGHT

She could not understand it.
By chance twice that day
    turning her head in backward glance,
    she glimpsed a bird perched on her shoulder.

That night, a cry — a devil's squeal,
    a beating at the upstairs window ledge,
    a clawing at the screen in crazed appeal.
Then in the moonlight, wings
    dizzied the eye angling across
    the bed, window to window,
    whirling frantically, and were lost.

      — John, a bird got in our room last night,
      — Oh, Lucy! . . .
        But *A spirit escaped*, she thought,
        And dreaded news.

Next week, two green flies
    fought at the attic window —
Something not freed —
    ensnared in its own flight. . . .
And a letter telling
    of a certain night —
    an old friend met at the airport
    by wife, psychiatrist,
    and plainclothesman. . . .
    "Our genius is doing well."

EIGHTIETH BIRTHDAY

Bee-legged, bee-spirited, preoccupied,
He stalks the churchyard,
The lifeless earth of hard good-byes:
School chum and cousin! . . .
You wouldn't know me now.
But I'd know you,
    My out-of-date young folks.
That first strange heedlessness was Brother's.
But I was young then, callous —
It was that last one. . . .
    Can it be, grass already?
One night she thought I stood her up.
A flash flood took the bridge;
She waited over there. All kisses
Never really set it right.
To be kept waiting. . . .
    Why do I dally now?
You, fence! — you, road! —
You, spot the ground humps by the holly tree!
How will you exist at twilight,
Without me here?
    Say I stay!
Why can't I say good-bye?
My hand turns for my woods —
My cheek yearns to my sky,
The candle snuffed, the light sped whence it came —
It's hard! and
I decline; in short, won't go.
In the mind's honeycomb are many dreams.
Shall all be sealed, and never a wind whip through?
The sun sets and the fields dissolve.
Now my date waiting in the dark says hungrily
Come to me, life, come to me. I need thee.

EPITAPH

She lies where doves call, bedded,
From the creek bank; creek bedded, too,
Willow and gum ruched honeysuckle;
The Saint graveyard's neglected.

Her house was screenless; doors stood wide;
Leaves drifted unwatched down the hall;
Hens left warm eggs indoors.
A stray lamb maddened by the scolding floor
Galloping broom to bed to wall to wall
Fell out the back door finally, prayers-answered.

For she was always in the low-grounds
Chopping cotton, or by the orchard
Binding wheat with wheat-strands,
Thinning the corn slips in the new-ground field,
Then home to snatch the coffee pot
Up off the floor (where the baby'd played),
Lay table, before they all got in.

— Kate, this brew's not fit to drink.
    — What? . . .
                Oh Lord.
— Don't cry, Kate
    — But I can't help it.
    I never cried for shirtwaists
    Or China cups
    Or crocheted pillow shams. I've not.
    But oh to have it said of me
    She boiled the gosling in the coffee pot . . .
        Poor gosling!

A FEW DAYS IN THE SOUTH IN FEBRUARY
(A Hospitality for S. K. Wightman, 1865)

> *Based on Mr. Wightman's account of his*
> *pilgrimage to North Carolina reprinted from*
> *family papers in* American Heritage *Feb-*
> *ruary 1963.*

1

One ship, one only
One sentry
One grave marked

An old man seeking a battlefield,
I march on the land of the enemy
For my son.
Who will know where he fell?
How take him, taken by the enemy?
How wrest him, young and strong
From war, from peace?

> *Your Christmas letter descended*
> *Like a Parrot shell and near*
> *Annihilated this home-starved soldier. . . .*
> Six days before!
> Climbing the parapet, a minie ball.
> His comrade's flask implored declining lips.

The battlefield stretches south.
Is it salt-marsh birds —
Or dead soldiers whistling?
Nightmare or real madness?
I stumble over dead grass locked in ice.

This alien wind blows sand
Not southern; arctic sand peppers
My flowing eyes and face.
I hear my wild voice singing hymns;

Feel tears like death-throes shake me,
Then breath gives out and I sit down to rest.
The salt wind roughs sand-wounds.
The eye calls, *Edward.* . . .
Answer, only those wind-borne birds.
Expanse of sea and marsh.
Expanse of dunes.

I hail the single soldier strolling near.
We two meet in an empty world.
    (Surely the bounds of fate,
    A grim tale's magic.)
"Graves from the battle of January 15?"
"On that knoll, sir."

    Surely the bounds of our lives
    Are fixed by our Creator.
    One marked, one only,
    The pine-stave written on in lampblack.
    My trembling spectacles give time for magic:
      Sergt Major
        3rd NYV
          E. K. Wightman

The darling of his sisters, mother
His steady eye, good sense
His quiet dreams
It seems I may spend out my years
Beside the spot.

I walk away,
Return and weep again.

Again I try to go on with my plan,
Set out for General Terry's —
Come back to him.

Three times I leave and
Stay to mourn.

So, thanking God for His
Mercy and goodness to me —
Only one grave marked.
Surely the bounds of our lives

2

Take up the body now?
Only a pine coffin? Ah.
At some future time. . . .
With one of lead. . . .
    Gentlemen, I must say
    Without intending to offend that
    (If it be not counter to God's will)
    I will never leave Federal Point
    Without Edward's body.

"If we had salt and rosin. . . .
"Things unsettled. . . ."
    Only to wait,
    Thanking God for His mercy and goodness:
    One ship, one only.
    One sentry,
    One grave marked.

    On the sealing of coffins. . . .
Salt in supply.
Tentcloth, none. No pitch nor rosin.

3

(Surely the bounds of fatè,
A grim tale's magic)
    No pitch   no rosin
Here near the tidewater is a knoll of sand.
I loiter,
Led by — the devil despair?
Godmother in disguise?
The hand of God?

Take this fragment of a pickax
And look there near the tidewater.
    Hans, or Abraham, obey.

To my astonishment. . . .
A barrel of rosin
There buried in the sand.
    Tears, thanking, etc.

I take the load upon my back
Struggling through deep sand
    (*Especially as . . . not at that time*
    In good health and not for years
    Subject to so great exposure)

Near nightfall, greatly fatigued,
I drift into a German fairy tale:
    Pity the sorrows of a poor old man
    Whose trembling limbs have borne him to your door. . . .

    "Orderly, take your horse and another;
    "Go with this gentleman to the Point."

And so aboard the *Montauk* for the night.

4

Needing what you don't want is hell.
A need for pitch, for sealing-black. . . .
Again stand at the magic spot
The Cape Fear's tide,
Conjure a barrel grounded in the shallows
Delightful as the ark in Pharaoh's flags
Delightful as the babe to Levi's house,
This coffin-gift.

The tide gone out, the barrel turns to staves —
Staves thick-pitched inside.
    Thanking God, etc. . . .

Beside the joiner's bench
I steady planks, his bed,
Give from my hand the separate coffin nails,
    Thanking God,

5

A tent-cloth, a detail of men,
A hollow in the sand, a fire,
Pitch and a little rosin in a pot.
It bubbles smackingly.
We frost the coffin and pitch tight the box,
Swab black the tent-cloth.

Unbidden blue coats straggle round
To meet my son.
I watch each salt of sand
On each gross shovel
Each inch to forty-eight,
Down to the end of miracles.

He lies half-turned,
His braided collar up
Against the elements (now chiefly earth)
Cape folded over face.
    Face . . . speeding from face to skull.
    (*The teeth appeared very prominent.*)

    What has your plum-pudding to do with me?
    Ah, my friends, thus it was with the captain
    In ancient times, when afar off he gazed
    At the smoking ruins
    Of the beloved city of his birth
    Burned by a barbarous enemy

In enemy land
Who mourns burned cities?
— Ruin!

Consider the holes made by the ball.
The hands, you judge, are very like. . . .
   ("Ah, can ye doubt?" asks one rough man,
   "For sure now, he greatly resembles ye")
   Face, white and swollen;
   Eyes, somehow injured.
   The wreck of our anticipations
   His love for me. . . .
   His Virgil parody. . . .
   "A favorite with the men"

        A puzzle, one set out so late
        Has overshot into eternity
        And left me plodding on.

At last I let them.
They wind the cloth about him.
And I, mounting, whip to Fort Lamb
Driven by the hammers.

Some days are pages ragtorn from hell.
Yet on this cruellest day night came.
Aboard the *Montauk*, water-rocked,
I slept, slept peacefully,
As if we two
Slept in our beds at home.

                6
His corpse recaptured from the enemy,
I brought him back where he was born
To that address his letters came.
   (*"To all — Dear Father   Mother   Fred
        Abbie and Jim   Chas
           Mary Ell   and
              Babies"*)

To services appropriately grave.
There lie in peace till Morning.
The sent-out child lies harvested.
The stone doves peck.

My watch ticks in my waistcoat.
My *News* waits by the window.
Snow falls
> *I believe that the bounds of our lives*
> *Are fixed by our Creator*
> *And we cannot pass them.*
> *The Lord gives and the Lord takes away*
> *Blessed be the name of the Lord.*

IV

IN THE BITTER ROOTS

THE PAINTED BRIDGE

It didn't seem like history. Seemed, more,
expediency. . . .

I'm walking to the beauty shop. On Rugby Road
a fractured fume of sodden leaf
and Phi Delts' pizza lunch, and through the pane
one of their rout white-coated, hands behind,
waits unattending in the wings, waits out
the weary midday to the coming night.

With harness creak of shoulder bag
I mount the railroad bridge, its college news
furled to the wall: day-in-and-day-out cries
in sky blue headlines on pea green BLANK DUKE;
blood red on U-Haul orange overnight
CONGRATS TO SHIRLEY MARILYN
ON PREMIERE OPENING.

                  A starchy stroke
whitewashes smut, then BE HEALTHY LOVE A NURSE
A PHI-NOMINAL YEAR AT U-V-A
and JJ as a bare rug (pink on gray).
I null it out.

A tomtom pulsing shakes the maple heads:
below me down the track the train comes on,
its big light blazing midday head-on course.
I've never in my life till now crossed when
a train was passing.

                  A striped-capped head
leans out the cab, an arm thrown all-out up
waves wildly.
— Never seen a woman cross a bridge before? —
His eager face ignites at happenstance, but
I hang fire.

And suffocating fumes
engulf the wavy birthday caps,
his carpe diem's capped by captioned bridge —
he's under.

I descend the railroad street.

Below the bridge the blue-lined buckets and
caked lids, the wares the news was made of,
litter the ditch's glittering careless depth.

I'm off. Off for my —   *set.*

THE GOING AWAY OF YOUNG PEOPLE
September 1, 1975

1

This was the day
The crumbs from last night's dinner
Lay all day on the table.

Your room filled only by sunlight
Is darkened by the late sleeper.

You forgot your love.
I'd mail it but
There's the chore of string
And paper and
The timbre of hi-fi turned off
Strings the psyche.

Anyway it's stuff I'm used
To stumbling over in various
Recesses of my house
Wondering why I haven't
Given it away, put it
To some use —
But keep on hoarding it, ashamed.

2

And our sailers-away hang yet full sail
In our autumn windows,
The windows across the street
Becalmed of young people.
Grass infiltrates their marigolds.
The garage cries out.

3

I won't say good-bye
But all leave-taking is a permanence.
We can't be sewed back up.
My mother's face at the window
Like a postage stamp
Hinges a faded September.

4

Windows between Septembers
More and more windows
Muffling, fogging over,
At last reflect only me
In car windows, kitchen windows,
Across-the-street-windows
This window I open over your bed
In case you should come back
For what we both forgot.

WOMEN'S TERMINAL WARD

she was walking the two white Spitzes
in the dusk of College Circle

       three wraiths
  dreaming absently of that female babe
  the chairman forbade that she adopt

she was waltzing into class late

       wobbling
under a giant amaryllis urn
rotating it on the desk egging it on
lost in its angles

    where to turn?

shelled with cancer
  faded hair sheeting the bellied
pillow in the veiled ward she wakes
  to her old students

      glows
  cherubic
go long! you girls oughtn't be kissing me
  we kiss her again
I have reaped where I have not sowed . . . .
  (night nurse running her soft legs off elsewhere)
we linger still

    grayly
  amaryllis
a little woozy *the bedpan please*
  the white duck shirttail the lifting hard
and the balding vulva the shell of daughters
  looms in this fleeing light
this manless ward

NEW DUST

Who was Athena's pet —
Be glad you're dead.
That you should see the shadow fleshen!
The shade caught in the arachnid net —

This dust was Randall and they say
That almost on his lucky day
He found his only luck to be
The dark concrete of 53

But I'm Athena's pet. . . .
Send me my jeweled bridle,
My Austrian sweater and more books. . . .
    Shaking off rejected Anteia
    I soared again
    Freed of that heaviness.
    I watched her fall into the human stars.
    What gods would take her part?
    She said they did.
    I wander in the Plain of Wandering
    In October, in full light of Pegasus
    Having repulsed the lady's love,
    Black man in blackness.

(My hoofs strike sparks from you —
I collect them in a basket
For my daughter.
    Empty the shelves!
I flew my library to Baltimore
And ate it.)

TO THE 15 BYPASS. . . .
    To be fifteen!
    Sabertooth at the Joint Library,
    Gnawing Fannie's knee. . . .
    Here by the laboring highway

[164]

With painful hands I strain . . .
With a bottle, but no spoon . . .
— "Let *that* be a medicine to you."
(I tell you it sure helps
to have some sympathy).

I draw towards HWY. 29.
Cars pass —   to —
To Greensboro —   that's home —
Lucy —   and supper. . . .
    A cruel cold snap.
    Not blackberry winter —
    Winter! and a white beard.
    Lost, those vernal altitudes,
    Clambering
    Past my last equinox.
    There was a time, I drove.
    (For the sin of surpassing
    They turned on him —
    The gods, the mount he rode.)

      But what if the story had been different?

    Mother said I had her eyes.
    What I'd give for my own! . . .

This dread is too dreadful

A car has two eyes
A windshield two faces

    For me, one unflowering autumn
    It went so ill that I

Two heads two headlights CAR

    Oh mother
    I've broken one of my immortal bones
    blind
    my immortal I

RACK AND RUIN

Only the taxi,
Impounding and freeing the companions.

Only a farm truck
Hogging the paved pigtrack,
Lightwashing the venetian blinds by night
From as far as the church.

Only the Southbound
Loping through the red cut,
Straddling the trestle at the creek,
The crossing bell spiring church dreams.

No thing more,
No person more,
Enters the house.

The granary is gone,
And the pastures forget.
Asparagus travels to
Unsanctioned lands.
(Red beads before soup.)

And she, my light,
Sees a darkness coming on,
Admiring her new shoes
Set innocently together,
Pushing her newly short white hair
With heavy coping hand —
Forgets what she was going to say,
Wonders why she is on the porch.

(And Whatever-Her-Name-Is
Comes to the tune
Of fifteen dollars a night
And picks the refrigerator bones.)
Shrugging like an embarrassed child —
My gray stuff's washed whiter than snow —
She rises daily more innocent
Of encumbrance and impedimenta.
Pressing transparent brow to the pane,
Elbows on sill, she gazes abroad,
Finds notes in her head:
    O I'm bound to carry
    My soul to the Lord.

WHEN ROBINS RETURN

When I see robins running in the grass
I wonder which he is, and if at last
he's as he wished, a robin in next life,
a shed eccentric, a wing-risen brass.

I wonder when I hear at dawn in May
that volubility at serious play
whether it's born verbal charm to tempt
earthworms, his Methodist constraint to pray,

or just a brisk happy advice to nests,
tutelage of the cuss and discuss
style, that taught more than we'd meant to learn,
from one who lived here wifeless and childless.

I see him flying with his lady mother
south, falls, to the Gulf. They doff their feathers
(at last she thinks him lyrical and bold)
evenings under magnolia weather,

play two-hand bridge, shuffling the red and black
cards with goldish talons. The fatal pack
is marked a different way this go-around:
justly, he'll eat her while she's fighting back.

VA. SUN. A.M. DEC. '73

morning mtns &
                    intersticial deer
sheets flick
wedding ring clicks
                    against the headboard
things are disappearing forever
     mtns. behind the mounting pines
     deer shot
     wedding rings flung in drawers
     Suns. no diff from rest of the wk.
     Va. no diff rest of the world

In dead-land nothing changes.

GIRL IN BLACK-STRIPED BATHING SUIT

The waves capsize,
    too blue by far.
Sea-weight jars
    the pier ties.
No sailing today.

There'll be no sailing anyway.
She's a compulsive something else,
the one who sits,
                the one,
on shore.

Since that girl in the black-striped
bathing suit first knelt, rapt,
on the diving board in my dreams,
days have become drier.
    Counting,
they wait for something.
Days that might walk alone, or
certainly, with a cane,
pull up the blankets to their eyes.
Sirens like Scheherazade
                    recite.

Days hear only the ringing in
the pillow, see only that girl
    staved in black stripes
kneel, bent in two.
Her flat locks lap with deja vu;
the days, staring, numb,
imagine themselves already damp.
I give her two years to jump.

LIMITS

Only he
Remembered the day we met
And only I
The day we said good-bye:
"Last day of June, our first blackberry pie,"
He always said.
A wood fire in the summer kitchen,
The hottest day. . . . A squall in the bedroom.
    I can't remember.

Nor he,
The December cube of clay,
The storm the day before,
How the bare trees
Played Giant Step in the dawn wind,
Or how
On the other bed, rhythmically
Touching her knuckles to the wall,
My mother slipped forever into fantasy.

Only he
Remembered the spoken hate
(Its change too sheepish to impart)
Saw daggers still growing
In bristling clump out of my heart.

I beg you, kids —   no memorials, please.
Don't write poems to me. Don't bother.
What we said we said. What's unsaid lacks ears.
In this I'm like my father.

TO FUTURE ELEANORS

How will you
cut off from Zions,
    fall on your knees among the lions?
What if you
cut off from hymns
    confound worksong with anthem

Cut off from Scripture
    find sense suspect
    and worship
        incoherence —
    distrust the laces
    and adore the tangled thread?

What of you
    without a holy thing,
    but every sacrilege
    of the sacrileged class?

Godsave your unsuspecting fists
grasping the fiery ladder bare,
your forehead
fighting a wordless solitaire.

Without some future language
how can I ask you?
If I could ask in Euphorese,
Moonskrit, in Ecolow. . . .

What will you do with
Grandma's savings —
those relics atticked
in your head
of effort, vision?

On pain of death, scratch pictures
in the dust
        as she did —
I fear my after-thirst.

A LITTLE OBITUARY

Last June the lovers took us walking
in Glendower churchyard after lunch
as if to soothe us: we too think of death.

Jogging together every day they stopped
short at the church too like a dwelling —
long windows securely wed to sill and door —
and there, aggressions eased, took hands and quoted
from Doctor Johnson and Voltaire over
aet. 20, Fell at Shiloh, Dearly Be
scratched off some moss, brushed back some trumpet vine
to peer into that dismal loss of loss.

His card today from Greece, hers, Oregon,
we propped together on the mantelpiece
upright rectangles crying jubilant elsewhere
to dead old orthodoxy jogging on.

OVER A STONE

But no call to get hot with me —
If he didn't want to help on
the stone why didn't he say so
when I first told him about the
hundred-dollar one for the two
    in smooth granite?
Why didn't he say so when she died
and he had them sing Rock of Ages
(because Whispering Hope was not a hymn)
and took the ivory-tipped sunshade
    and the old sword?
Why didn't he say so when I
was there doing the farming,
turning her every day, plates in
and slopjars out? And after that
when I walked the five miles to visit
setting out in morning shadows
waiting to leave till dark cooled the road
taking my breeches for his wife to mend
(The whole day, she had, and sometimes
I'd be still waiting there by lamplight)?
Even before that, why didn't he
speak up when Papa died and I
was there with Mother and the debt,
the Ford jacked up to save the tires?
Or walking through the woods to school,
I wearing his big outgrown shoes? When we
both got switched for the sugarbowl
    and cried plenty?
Why didn't he say so, back there,
when we slept together under
those heavy, cold, pants-and-coats quilts
one headboard for the two of us?
    Why did he wait?

LOVE KNOWS

Love knows but one story.
It sits in the corner with its book
and reads it over and over
lips parted, eyes shining —
how the face appeared at the window
    how the door was opened
        the eyes met
            and the hands

Luckily, it is my story.

ORDER AND LAW

A dog-cat yowling from the night,
a caterwauling to the gods
(cat-gods and tigers of that blood)
the animal trip-trigger yell
in raw extremity —   fanged to
the flesh, to tears. She hated.
The snarls drew her bared teeth down tight;
her flashlight shivering along
the hurried fences, she hated.

She heard it stop, like breath cut off.

Then yelp and blow, and blow and yelp,
bay-howl for mercy. Were the thuds
a stick, or fist, against the hide?

To the back door screaming, she clawed
into the dark from her black watch.
Stop that   Stop it   Stop Stop Stop

> And like an echo a frightened,
> woman's voice far on the spot
> injected in the blows   *stop it.*

It stopped.
A thrashing silent storm
    above the night:
above eviscerated cat,
unconscious dog, self-sickened man —
    and vicious self.
She had a nameless pressing pain —
a shooting pain in wrist.
                    Each beast
of earth made after his own kind —
made beast, made lurching prey, made
    fatal shots that missed.

NEW GIRLS

Devious, devious are
primroses in shade
collecting sunshine
without sunshine.
Sprawling on the grass
they grip their books.
The strings of summer
ring without answer.
Hello Juliana?
Hello Augusta?
What are you doing tomorrow?
Sleeping,
         sleeping.

Numerous the shades
under primroses,
shifting sands and
sets and seasons,
reaching for the
fellow pillow,
reaching for the
strings of summer,
too treble, too shining
for inside eyes.

IN CASE OF DANGER

                                 I am sending my son
an emergency survival kit:
                                 flares
to light up wild mountainous terrain to
searchers in planes;
                                 inscrutably furled
space blanket, tested against exposure
at Everest by recent explorers;
small high-calorie ration to sustain
one really strayed to the edge of the world.
I include a candle for him to set
in a can of sand in the car. I have
read just so much heat will keep a stranded
                                 motorist from freezing.

My son lives quietly, mostly browsing
in libraries in Iowa City,
lingering sometimes late at a bar
amberizing Freud and Philip Levine
with his friends; occasionally he
spends a morning at the laundromat.

    But once when four he ran headlong
    towards the edge of an unrailed deck
    in LeHavre; a ship's guard jumped in front.
    I was wearing a tissue wool suit
    and brown hat.
                    I had to sit down.
    Again, at ten alarmed us all
    rising to chart Jupiter's moons —
    at four A.M., when a straggler
    might have entered the dark house, or
    he been molested by a milkman.

In London when he was so ill
I watched sea birds at sunrise flap
along the Thames beyond the obelisk,
and sick with fright by the deranged cot
prayed for this safe time.

I must write a letter of instructions:
                    When in Himalayas. . . .

RACHEL PLUMMER'S DREAM
Winter 1836

You never shut your eyes.
You always looked.

At the grizzled scalp you somehow recognized
even without the blue eyes and mustache,
through your blood that was Like to Strangle you
lying face down, tied,
    through the mass beating.

After five days without a Mouth of Food —
days of silence —   slogging —   stamina —
part of the skinclad band to the high timber,
you could not but Admire the Countrey
though short of breath from fasting, burdened with
your unborn baby, tentskins on your back.

You never turned your head
    from Little Pratt's
                calling,
   drawn from you.

When the unborn, born in captivity,
let live a week or so, was made their sport,
bounced on the frozen ground till lifeless,
you held your arms for it   and somehow
breathing new life in it, fired their new rage.
    You watched it   on a rope
whirled out by braves aponyback
till shredded on the cactus,
then thrown into your lap, a tattered mass,
and buried tearless with your hands and prayers
of thanks for its release.

You breathed the Purest Are you ever breathed
those snowy summits, Admired the Timber,
the Fine Springs, the Snow Rabbitt, undefiled —
(your fingers scarred with dressing hides, your feet
black-bitten) counted the advances of
the antelope, their turns, noting their
diminishing proximity, ghostly escape:
mused at the buffalo grazing in
the phantom sea —   it was "a sort of gas."

Bound to see, you crashed the powwow, ignored
their cuffs —   a dog that *would*, spoke Indian,
heard Indian —   *save* one white curse
a fat-mouthed Beadie sought you out to give —
ate roots Stol'n from the Mouse's Holes,
refused the serving of roast enemy; it was a foot.

You burned to see —   as for example,
the inside of those mountain caves
before decamping;
I see you all wrapped up
    dipping flax wicks
into some tallow got from buffalo —
with these your makeshift candles and firewood,
a flint —   with your young mistress took the Pieded Horse
on the uprising trail.
        Inside,
she took quick fright (she smelled the water)
but you would not go back.

Again, where it got dark, you struck the light,
and the splendor blinded.
She cried out, threatening you.
You slugged her with a stick of wood, wrestled,
• ready to kill her for the sight
that was to come.

By some odd chance, your light knocked to the ground
burned on. You took it up, squinted —
the cave burst into light, imperative. But first
you led her, tamed, the miles back to the mouth;
at last made your long way in that unearthly
twinkling dark, beside the crystal river,
to sound of mighty falls ahead,

                              plunging
how far?   into what unknown place?
    caught echoes of your dying baby's cries;
like tranced Ezekiel in Babylon
    descried the noise of wings, of wings let down —
though briers and thorns be with thee, not afraid!

and a Human Being came   comforting
releasing   balming   transfusing. . . .
Your captors, waiting at the mouth, half gave you up.

How analyze
    this parapsychologic episode
    this spiritual hiatus where
you closed your eyes a whole day and a night,
on through a second day? —
                         I discount sex.
So worn, half-starved, and suicidal —
    they say, consumptive, too.
The realist, you painted not at all.

I see him, see his gifts. He chose: to bathe
your wounds that never pained again,
that Resurrection flaring in the cave,
those stars in earth, time stopped
and you with eyes to see.

IN THE BITTER ROOTS

One who's never crossed the Mississippi
and never will, now —
how can I think I stand too
in that place
in Clark's stupendous mountains
escape unsure
thinking myself, too
part of a world cut off, receding?
They think me dead;
I fight, still, in this death,
these crossed meridians.
　　　"If we should git bewildered
　　　in these mountains —"

What, never to find
the River that Scoalds All the Others,
never present (the faithful buffoon) medals
to the tribes of Jefferson's red children?
to know unseen the Bitter Roots,
the Head that pained me not so much as yesterday?
to scratch my name, first vandal,
on Pomp's Pillar — ?

Only to stand watching
the chimneys take the sun,
no sponge dry enough for the tears,
no bowl adequate for the mixed feelings,
only — she standing at the window
by the gulf
trapped in these mountains
trapped in this face,
bewildering decay,
like him without one prayer,
one begging phrase
blown toward Virginia and native gods.

Can I think to find
a past, a past self, in these passes,
in hospital at Sevastapol,
following among Comanche squaws?
Yes, and more,
I proceed without a guide
at this stage of the expedition
though it's known madness.

ACKNOWLEDGMENTS

The author and publisher wish to thank the following periodicals
for permission to reprint certain poems.

Paris Review for "No"; *Shenandoah* for "On the Writing of Poems"
and "In the Echoes, Wintering"; *Triquarterly* for "Short Foray";
Key West Review for "Hatchways" and "Dog in *The Quiet Man*";
Grand Street for "At the Altar" and "Next Year"; *The Boston Review* for
"No Need" (June 1989); *Partisan Review* for "March 9" (first published
in vol. 53, no. 4, 1986); *Seneca Review* for "Harvest, 1925,"
"A Permanent Dye," and "Boiled Peanuts"; "Balance Brought Forward"
originally appeared in the January 16, 1989 issue of *The New Yorker*;
The Virginia Quarterly Review for "Enter Daughter";
The Kenyon Review for "The Altar Needlework," "How Morning Comes,
Out of Sleep," and "The Sunny Day"; *The Southern Review* for "Escaped,"
"The Green house," "Pain in the House," and "Gainesville, March";
and Palaemon Press Ltd, from its *New and Selected Poems*
by Eleanor Ross Taylor, published 1983, for the poems in II. Wilderness of
Ladies, III. Welcome Eumenides, and IV. In the Bitter Roots
in the present volume.